WHEN AMERICA WINS
THE WORLD CUP

SHIFTING THE SPORTS CULTURE

MATTHEW KOLESKY

WHEN AMERICA WINS THE WORLD CUP
SHIFTING THE SPORTS CULTURE

iUniverse books may be ordered through booksellers or by contacting:

iUniverse LLC
1663 Liberty Drive
Bloomington, IN 47403
www.iuniverse.com
1-800-Authors (1-800-288-4677)

ISBN: 978-1-4917-3694-4 (sc)
ISBN: 978-1-4917-3695-1 (hc)
ISBN: 978-1-4917-3696-8 (e)

Library of Congress Control Number: 2014910330

Printed in the United States of America.

iUniverse rev. date: 10/24/2014

FOREWORD

Finally, the United States of America is a soccer nation! Yes, the USA is just as crazy as other countries across the globe and the sport continues to grow at home. More importantly, this growth will continue for decades to come. During the 2014 Brazil World Cup, people gathered everywhere crowding streets, stadiums, restaurants and bars to cheer for Team USA. America shared something amazing, and witnessed the colorful joy delivered through The Beautiful Game. The passion is very much alive. It is evident through the emergence of the American Outlaws (AO) fan club that began in 2007. From a small group of diehard soccer fans in Lincoln, Nebraska, AO now links American soccer fans all over the world. I know, who would have ever thought Lincoln, Nebraska? I have family that lives in Lincoln and they tell me the city that once only saw red now sees a red, white and blue rainbow. Real football is alive and kicking everywhere.

It is not a coincidence that America's sporting elite have made huge investments, buying teams and building stadiums for Major League Soccer (MLS). These same investors realize the US has a large, untapped soccer market and have purchased big clubs around the world. Manchester United, Arsenal, Tottenham Hotspurs are all owned by Americans. Even NBA star LeBron James, one of America's greatest athletes, bought a minority share of Liverpool in

2011. Liverpool is majority owned by the Fenway Sports group, the same group that owns Major League Baseball's legendary franchise, the Boston Red Sox as well as Roush Fenway Racing of NASCAR.

Now that the USA has become a soccer nation, the time has arrived for America to raise the bar and achieve the ultimate goal, winning the FIFA World Cup. Matthew Kolesky is the brilliant creator and author of When America Wins the World Cup. Matthew creatively navigates us through the most memorable moments of US Soccer and brings to life the hope, the possibility, and reality for USMNT to win the FIFA World Cup. He shares his real life stories as a fan and provides a look at the US team and what to expect for the quest to become #1 in the world. This book is special. This is a book that enhanced my passion for soccer.

Since I was seven years old, I have dedicated my life to reaching the highest level of play and to make a difference in building soccer in America. I am forever grateful to have played professionally in the German Bundesliga, Major League Soccer, the Olympics, the 1990 Italy FIFA World Cup and 1994 USA FIFA World Cup. After retirement from the LA Galaxy I was honored to be inducted as the first MLS player in the US National Soccer Hall of Fame. Then, leading up to the 2014 Brazil FIFA World Cup, Sports Illustrated deemed my World Cup qualifying goal versus Trinidad and Tobago as the "Most Significant Goal" ever scored in United States soccer history. Soccer is a team sport, so it's most important for me to thank all those that were supportive and helped with my personal success. Thank you to my family, my friends, teammates, US Soccer, my opponents, and the fans. This would have never been possible without all of you. The Beautiful Game has been so wonderful to me and has given me a global perspective of people and life. Having been fortunate to play the game at the highest of levels, and see the world while playing and living my childhood dream, today I strive for more ways to make a difference. This is the very reason "When America Wins the World Cup" holds a special place in my heart. The book is an extremely touching testament that brings to life the possibility that the United States Men's National Team will one day win the FIFA World Cup. It is real! Thank you Matthew for keeping the hope alive!

Go USA! Unite and Strengthen.
And Keep Kicking.
Paul Caligiuri

PREFACE

Today's headline reads, "Stars and Stripes Wins the FIFA World Cup."

The United States of America Men's National Team affirmed their number-one world ranking as they hung on to win the 20_ _ World Cup. Elite footballing nations have a new member as the USMNT raised the trophy in Sydney. US head coach Michael Bradley said after the game, "Thank you for all the hard work from the players and fans. We have vanquished the global perception that the United States doesn't play football. This win is for all soccer fans, players, parents, and supporters of US Soccer who have dreamed of this day!" Two strikes from Ballon d'Or winner Morten Johnson in the first half stood up as the Stars and Stripes withstood a late fury mounted by the Red Devils.

Yes, the author is now awake. The headline above begs the questions: What year is the headline? Will it happen in my lifetime? Maybe 2022, 2030, or beyond? I'd like to think so.

Other questions to consider from the headline: Why is Australia hosting a World Cup? The USMNT is number one in the world and they have a Ballon D'Or winner? I know. I know. But what can I say other than "Dream big or go home"?

Globally, men dominate the sport of soccer, but the USMNT has never dominated. If we are to win the World Cup, the sports culture in America will need to continue its shift in soccer's direction. The aim of this book is to ride the growing American soccer wave and humbly enhance it. I will look at the history of the sport through what I consider significant mileposts in the development of the game in America. Included are some of my experiences as a fan as well as those of other fans. They are here to illustrate to my fellow Americans that we can be passionate and embrace the global game. The sport is building again in America, and the rest of the world is slowly starting to realize that we are taking soccer seriously at the national level.

Also included are a few gentle educational sections to help the American reader gain a deeper understanding of the game. I hope you read it and are then inspired to go to a match. I hope you are inspired to click the remote and watch MLS instead of bowling or basketball.

My only credentials for writing, aside from being an advocate for American soccer and a fan, come from coaching soccer in Alaska for several years and then obtaining my Level 1 FA (Football Association) coaching certification in England and putting it into practice at the youth levels in the Southwest London County of Surrey.

Some of the inspiration for writing this book came from *Fever Pitch* by Nick Hornby. It follows one man's honest lifelong journey as an Arsenal supporter. He wanted to tell his story, the candid tale of a pure fan. While reading it, I realized that so many Americans share his passion for the game, but nobody, domestically or internationally, seemed to understand this outside of American soccer circles. Other inspiration came from many Britons and Europeans who seem to think the quality of US players is still where it was thirty or forty years ago.

The book is also about continuing the quest for respect of US Soccer at home and around the world. Most importantly, it's about what every American soccer fan wants: to see the Men's Stars and Stripes win the World Cup. Is that ambitious? That's America.

In case you aren't yet familiar with football terms and acronyms, I will provide a handy reference section:

- Football (or soccer, futbal, futbol, or *il calcio* in Italy) is the premier sport for most nations across Europe, South America, most of Africa, Asia, and Central America. I will use soccer and football interchangeably and sometimes will refer to football as American football. The transition will take time and may be painful for some Americans. Get used to seeing football used for soccer and futbol.
- USMNT is the United States Men's National Team.
- USWNT is the United States Women's National Team.
- WCQ is World Cup Qualifier, a match that counts toward playing in the next World Cup Finals.
- World Cup Finals is the tournament known around the world as the World Cup. Thirty-two nations qualify for the tournament.
- CONCACAF is the Confederation of North, Central American, and Caribbean Association Football. This is the confederation for the United States, Mexico, Jamaica, Costa Rica, Honduras, Canada, and any other country in North or Central America and the Caribbean.
- MLS is Major League Soccer, the top level of soccer in the United States and Canada.

- EPL is English Premier League or Barclay's Premier League, the top level of soccer in England and Wales. (I've started a petition to rename the league the "Barclay's Mostly English and a Wee Bit Welsh Premier League," as Swansea City was joined by fellow Welsh club Cardiff City for the 2013–2014 season.) Scotland and Northern Ireland play in their own sandboxes.
- UEFA is the Union of European Football Associations.
- Pitch is the field.
- Match is a game.
- Courgette is a zucchini.
- Torch is a flashlight.
- Derby (pronounced "darby") is a rivalry match, usually in the same town or locale.
- The Hex, or Hexagonal Playoffs, is the name of the final round of qualifying for the World Cup in the CONCACAF.
- Caps means playing in a game for your national team. For some fans, it means attending an international game.
- FC is football club, as in Barcelona FC.
- Stars and Stripes is the nickname for the US national soccer teams.
- Ballon d'Or is the trophy given to the best football player in the world each year.

INTRODUCTION

Into stoppage time, the game is still undecided. Deep near the box, a midfielder sends in a cross past the far post. A decent shot is taken, but the ball settles to the goalkeeper, who knows he needs to push play the other direction quickly. He launches a long NFL-worthy pass to a winger, which moves the play downfield on a break. A cross comes in toward the goal, and a sliding shot is put right at the keeper. The rebound falls to Landon Donovan, and he buries it.

The defenders collapse. The goalie is furious. Some players have faces buried in hands as the crowd erupts. The American players dog-pile in celebration. It's a stoppage time victory: USA 1–0 Algeria. One goal can be epic, life-changing, and life-affirming. It's redemption.

That goal was a pivotal moment in US Soccer history. The world was watching. America was watching. As the remaining ninety seconds of injury time ticked off, that goal put the United States at the top of its World Cup group after the third and final game, ahead of England, Algeria, and Slovenia at the 2010 World Cup. It forever changed the trajectory of the sport in America as it bolstered an already growing MLS and interest in soccer in America. It was David and Victoria Beckham coming to America ten times over. Well, okay, maybe it was three or four Sir Becks and Posh Spice American invasions. (Seriously, David Beckham isn't knighted yet? It's only a matter of time.) After decades of being an up-and-coming sport in America with starts, stops, retrenchment, and the perpetual rebooting of a national league, that was the moment when soccer truly arrived in the American collective consciousness.

The sport is securing itself in the national culture. It can't possibly go backward. The MLS is growing, and in 2014, the World Cup was broadcast live from Brazil to America in prime time.

I couldn't say it better. USMNT Coach Jurgen Klinsmann, after the United States hoisted the Gold Cup in Chicago on July 28, 2013, said, "I think soccer in this country is unstoppable. You can't stop it anymore. It will only get better. It will get bigger. You know the crowds we had in the last… Games like sixty, seventy, eighty thousand you know in Dallas and Baltimore. People are buying into the sport. Millions of kids playing in this country."[1]

It continues to build.

---

[1] http://www.ussoccer.com/mens-national-team/tournaments/2013-concacaf-gold-cup

PART 1

CHAPTER ONE

Where We Were: An Abridged History of Soccer in America

I AM NOT A soccer historian, but the devolution and subsequent modern evolution of the sport in America intrigues me. I am highlighting significant milestones that ultimately elevated the game into a stable and growing position in American society and helped shift the mind-set of American soccer around the world. The wreckage of teams and leagues, some from a bygone era, with rich history to modern disasters, litter the landscape.

I've engaged with many folks across the pond and around Europe. The response I get from Brits and Europeans is predictably the same, particularly when I mention the history of the sport in America.

"You're writing a book about American soccer?"

"That won't take long."

Knee slapping and chuckling follows. Sadly, our soccer history is forgotten at home and abroad, lost to the annals of time. While researching this book, I ran across glimpses of the sport in early America, Boston, New York, and New Orleans as immigrants brought the game with them. As America tried to distance itself from the British and European countries, we set off on new cultural courses.

1

That being said, we can find the game being played in America well over 150 years ago, and it has a rich, partially buried history. Bit by bit, researchers, historians, fans, and modern MLS teams looking to connect with and honor the past are digging it up.

Going back a bit farther, there are reports about Native Americans playing a game, and the US Soccer website has a great timeline with the first entry from 1620.

> American folklore asserts that Pilgrim Fathers, upon settling at Plymouth Rock found American Indians along the Massachusetts coast playing a form of soccer. The Indians called it "Pasuckquakkohowog," which means "they gather to play football."[2]

Next, we travel to the mid-nineteenth century. It was a turbulent time in America with the Civil War raging. Soccer was being played, and the game's popularity grew as immigrants from Britain and Ireland continued to arrive, bringing a type of early soccer with them. The first official football club in the United States was the Oneida Club, formed in Boston in 1862. They never allowed a goal in the four seasons of playing. On the monument in Boston commemorating the team, it reads, "On this field the Oneida Club of Boston, the first organized football club in the United States, played against all comers from 1862 to 1865 - The Oneida goal was never crossed."[3]

Although they get credit, these guys didn't play soccer as we know it today. Similar to the early English game, there were no formal, standardized rules for playing. It was violent, and grudges were often carried out on the field.

---

[2]   www.ussoccer.com

[3]   www.celebrateboston.com/first/football-club.htm

This early game, including the style played by Oneida, looked more like rugby than modern soccer. So how can they hold claim to the first official club in the States? Like anything standing the test of time, it was well documented. They kept a roster as well as records detailing the matches played. Not so well documented are other glimpses of the sport surfacing in New Orleans around the same time. While the game was being played in the United States in the late 1800s, we have to go to England in 1863 to find the origins of the modern game.

Roots of Modern Football

Rugby and soccer have the same ancestry, split from the same game once the "I want to use my hands" folks were separated from the "We want to kick the ball" folks in 1863 across the pond by a group of English teams. Trying to establish a system of rules to govern sport, a group of representatives from local FCs met on October 26, 1863, "for the purpose of forming an Association with the object of establishing a definite code of rules for the regulation of the game."[4]

This is considered to be the defining moment in the development of the modern game and sent it on firm footing to expand around the world with the British Empire as well as to other parts of the globe, including Brazil and Spain. It's good to see rule of law works well when applied to sports. It's uniform, standardized, and consistent. Did they come up with Big Macs and the Model T as well?

Using 1863 as a starting point, the game began to evolve. Reading about the first real football, you can see that things certainly have changed. My notes have been included in the brackets.

"Football," they thought, would be a blend of handling and dribbling. [Maybe the FA should be credited with starting basketball as well.] Players would be able to handle the ball: a fair catch accompanied by "a mark with the heel" would win a free kick. [I have no idea what this means. Perhaps something was lost from the original translation from Middle English: Whan that playen wel cathe and handl'd the ball, to take in tyme a foot into the groond.]

The sticking point was "hacking," or kicking an opponent on the leg, which Blackheath FC wanted to keep. [Yes, kicking and hacking others! What a glorious sport. Why did this take so long to catch on in America? We have professional wrestling.] The laws originally drafted by Morley were finally approved at the sixth meeting, on 8 December, and there would be no hacking. They were published by John Lillywhite of Seymour Street in a booklet that cost a shilling and sixpence. [The FA began down that treacherous, money-grubbing road very early.] The FA was keen to see its laws in action [read as ordered by Queen Victoria], and a match was played between Barnes and Richmond at Limes Field in Barnes on 19 December. It was a 0–0 draw. [How appropriate some in America might say!][5]

---

[5]   www.thefa.com

I found myself connected to the history more than I realized. My younger son plays for a local club team in Richmond called the Kew Park Rangers, and on Saturday, October 26, 2013, he had practice like every other Saturday. However, one particular coach that morning remembered the significant day 150 years earlier when the FA was established. He went on and mentioned the first official game of "football" played in the world under the new rules took place just down the road from where we had been practicing.

While the American colonialists may have moved on culturally in some aspects from Mother England, commonwealth sports initially took hold. Soccer, as the game was played back then, dominated American sports in the mid- to late 1800s along with rowing. It was a different age. Gradually, we invented new sports and shunned tea. Baseball, basketball, and American football rose to take over the consciousness of the 1900s, and we imported ice hockey from Canada.

American football traces its roots back to soccer and rugby as well. Walter Camp amended rugby's rules to include the downs as we know them today. He is credited with being the father of American football. Still, the connection to rugby can be seen most clearly in the term "touchdown." In rugby, a try is scored when the players cross the goal line and then touches the ball down to the ground, hence "touchdown". Both modern soccer and American football have eleven players on the field at any given time. Some modern American soccer fans take issue with the term "football" used to describe a game in which most plays the foot doesn't touch the ball. Even the author uses "football" and "soccer" interchangeably in this book.

In 1913, the United States of America Foot Ball Association was established in New York. This organization is today the governing body in the United States for soccer, and it is now called the US Soccer Federation that just celebrated it centenary.

The US Open Cup

With the establishment of a national governing body to provide structure and support to the sport, the United States of America Foot Ball Association also held the first US Open Cup. In 1914, the Brooklyn Field Club won in the final over Brooklyn Celtic in Pawtucket, Rhode Island.

> At long last the moment had arrived, the crowning of first ever National Challenge Cup champion. On October 12, 1913, the list of 40 participating teams was announced, and on November 1 the first games were played. Almost six months later, Brooklyn Celtic and Brooklyn Field Club emerged the sole survivors of the elimination contests, convening at Coats Field in Pawtucket, Rhode Island to decide who would reign supreme and lift the Dewar Challenge Trophy. The Pawtucket Times described the scene at Coats Field that afternoon: "Long before the captains had met in the center of the field... every vantage point within the spacious enclosure was peawed with humanity. The grandstand and bleachers filled like magic; around the field the spectators thronged seven and eight deep. Every automobile was filled to its capacity and even the baseballs scoreboard in left field provided a precious foothold for groups of hardy souls. Thomas Bagnall, president of the New York Amateur Association Football League, USFA President Dr. Rudolph G.

Manning, and USFA Secretary Thomas Cahill were all on hand for this historic occasion, the crowning of the first true soccer champion of the United States. After both teams were photographed and a "moving picture machine" was set up in the grandstand to film the action, Celtic forward Thomas Campion kicked off at 3:21 pm.[6]

The competition has grown over the past 10 years. Now, MLS teams can compete for the US Open Cup, as can just about any other team. It is in the same spirit as an open golf or tennis tournament, that is, amateur teams can gain access.

Bethlehem Steel FC

Soccer began to take hold around the country in the early 1900s, and no team was as successful as Bethlehem Steel FC. Again, I found myself connected to the American soccer past through my grandfather. It all goes back to driving around the dilapidated steel mills in Bethlehem, Pennsylvania, with him. I saw the old blast furnaces, the cooling areas, and the history. He talked about working at Bethlehem Steel with guys with named Stuffy, Reds, and Chico. They all worked and smoked together. I saw images of red-faced workers with cigarettes dangling from the mouths and each with strong jaw lines. It was back when working for a living meant rolling up your sleeves and making something tangible, components to a high-rise or a navy warship.

Now, the old derelict buildings of Bethlehem Steel seem to go on for miles. He'd point and say things like, "See that building with the hole in the roof? That was where they cooled the steel. They'd

---

[6]   www.thecup.us

spray chemicals on them, and most of the guys in that job didn't last very long."

He worked in the steel mills, and he played soccer. When my grandfather was in junior high in Bethlehem, they won the city football championship, and the team decided to repeat the grade so they could win it again. And they did. The game was important to them. Reflecting on my time with my grandfather before his passing made me realize that he was a connection to the past for me, to my family, my history, and football in America.

From 1912–1930, Bethlehem Steel FC dominated the American soccer landscape. This team represented the iconic American company. Bethlehem Steel FC is one of the most storied soccer teams in American history, winning multiple league trophies and cups, including the American Cup (now called the US Open Cup). And they even toured Europe.

The Philadelphia Union paid tribute to Bethlehem Steel FC (BSFC), remembering those great teams from the early 1900s. In 2013, the Union unveiled a third kit further honoring the BSFC. The Union's website hits the nail on the head.

> "Professional soccer has a dormant but rich history in the Greater Philadelphia region dating back over 100 years," said Sakiewicz. "Our vision with this concept is to revive the history and recognize the past. As the Philadelphia Union now leads professional soccer into the 21st century it is our duty and responsibility to remember, honor and pay tribute to those teams that came before us and

laid the groundwork for the growth of the game in the region."[7]

It is a great legacy for the Philadelphia Union to associate with and can help drive their brand while telling a great American soccer story. The connections to the past are there, and they go back farther than the NBA and NFL. We just have to do a little digging.

Early American History in the World Cup

The USMNT played in the inaugural 1930 World Cup hosted by eventual winner Uruguay. It was a competition devoid of several of the European powers, but the United States nonetheless finished third, which included a 3–0 win over Paraguay and saw the first ever World Cup hat trick, scored by American Bert Patenaude. Aside from Paraguay, Belgium was in our group, and we dispatched them 3–0 as well, making it to the knockout stage but only to get lambasted by Argentina 6-1.

In 1950, the American team played in the World Cup in Brazil. We lost to Spain 3–1 in our opening game, although the score line wasn't indicative of the match. We scored in the seventeenth minute and tried to hang on, only to have Spain score three times after the eightieth minute. Our next match was the shocker, 1–0 over England. This is still considered one of the biggest upsets in American soccer history. A group of ragtag American laborers who happened to play football took on the established professionals of England and won. However, Chile dispatched the United States from the World Cup in the final group game by 5–2, sending the

---

[7]   http://www.philadelphiaunion.com/news/2013/02/new-season-new-kit-union-uniform-upgrade-honors-soccers-deep-roots-philadelphia-area

United States into a long soccer winter. We wouldn't qualify for another World Cup for forty years.

The Goal that brought us back.

While soccer languished domestically, the international game continued to evolve and advance, and it would take thirty-nine years for our national team to make waves on the international scene. This barren, uncompetitive era helped foster skepticism, home and abroad, of American soccer. Some of it was deserved, as Americans focused on the national pastime and American football. The rise of the NFL captured the hearts and souls of Americans, even if the game never caught on outside North America.

The United States finally qualified for the 1990 World Cup hosted by Italy as we slogged through formidable regional competition and barely emerged. It wasn't without controversy though. Mexico had a very talented team and had been harshly disqualified for fielding ineligible players on their U-20 team, and as a result, CONCACAF and FIFA suspended all Mexican teams from all international competition for two years which helped ease the road for the USMNT.

Conspiracy theories abound that FIFA played a hand. Mexico was quite strong, and if they had been included in the qualifying group stages, it would have made our road in 1990 extremely difficult.

FIFA's website talks about the game that ended the forty-year drought. Going into the last WCQ, "soccer was of only nominal concern to most Americans in 1989."[8] We were away to Trididad and Tabago who only needed a draw to secure a World Cup birth and knock out the USMNT. T&T were ready to join the party.

---

[8]   http://www.fifa.com/associations/association=usa/news/index.html

But there was far more at stake for the USMNT than just qualifying for a FIFA World Cup for the first time in 40 years. The US Soccer Federation was deeply in the red and nearing bankruptcy. The biggest concern spreading was that the U.S. might lose the hosting rights for FIFA World Cup 1994, mainly because Americans lacked interest in soccer and the possibility that the U.S. wouldn't qualify for Italia 1990. This was a heavy burden for the young and inexperienced US team. On November 19, 1989, the last of all global world cup qualifiers would take place in the Caribbean, and the world was anxiously waiting to see which team would earn the 24th and final spot for the Coppa del Mondo FIFA Italia '90. Trinidad and Tobago intentionally scheduled the game for a mid-day kickoff. It was very hot and humid and they believed that would give them the advantage over the American side. On this day, the USMNT would change the course of American soccer forever. The US would go on to upset the highly favored home team 1-0. This day in the sun opened a gateway for unprecedented soccer growth and the game has prospered at every level since, including opportunities for TV, corporations, and investors to tap into the last and greatest football frontier, the United States.

Paul Caligiuri was an unlikely starter and defender. He was assigned to the center midfield duty and had explicit instructions to mark out Russell Latapy, Trinidad's playmaker, and not to go forward to risk counter attacks. In the 29th minute, that would all change. Caligiuri pushed the ball forward to initiate an attack, he then beat the on rushing defender, and shot a 35 yard left footed volley with top spin that dipped into the far left corner of the goal, scoring what has been deemed by Sports Illustrated "the most significant goal in U.S soccer history".[9] This victory not only put

---

[9]   http://www.si.com/longform/soccer-goals/goal1.html

us back in the World Cup but solidified the US hosting rights for the 1994 FIFA World Cup and paved the way for modern success.

Coming Back to America

Before the success of the 1994 World Cup, soccer started to emerge back into the mainstream culture. Glimpses of the game began to appear. Thankfully, television played a large part in getting Americans interested again. And don't we love a good story on TV? The BBC broadcasted the 1966 World Cup, won and hosted by England, to the States. England dramatically defeated West Germany 4–2 to claim the title of world champions. Then in 1970, Pelé played in his final World Cup and dazzled south of our border. Mexico hosted the World Cup, and the time slots were perfect for broadcasting the matches to the States.

In 1974, Pelé retired from his club, Santos, and the New York Cosmos, Steve Ross, and Henry Kissinger lured him to America. It was another milestone in US Soccer history, and it was a coup. Brazilians didn't want to see a national treasure head to America. However, news of Pelé's retirement hadn't gone unnoticed elsewhere, as general manager of the New York Cosmos Clive Toye explains. "Real Madrid and Juventus were sniffing around, so I said, 'If you go to Real or Juventus, all you could win is another championship, whereas if you come with us, you could win a country.'"[10]

Incredibly, the New York Cosmos assembled an all-star team of players. They were the first truly international superstar sports team. It's Lionel Messi, Cristiano Ronaldo, Eden Hazard, RVP, and Xavi all playing for the same club. Or it's the 1992 American Dream Team that dazzled the world at the Barcelona Olympics. Pelé, Beckenbauer, Cruyuff, and the enigmatic Italian tornado, Giorgio

---

[10] http://www.shortlist.com/entertainment/the-new-york-cosmos-comeback

Chinaglia, were drawing move than seventy thousand fans to games, and it was a party.

But it wasn't to be. The New York Cosmos and the North American Soccer League (NASL) played their last seasons in 1984. America wasn't quite ready.

America also showed that it can be fickle, and sadly, they folded like a cheap suit and went bust like New Coke. What the world learned of the soccer culture in America was that we needed the superstar name recognition. Otherwise, we weren't interested.

The New York Cosmos were the best and worst of America. What the Cosmos can bring back is their global brand recognition. They certainly won't be getting Ronaldo or Messi in their prime, but they will be able to build a stable team and compete at a high level again. They recently signed a deal with Emirates Airlines, sponsors of European heavyweights AC Milan, Paris St. Germain, and Arsenal. Heck, even Harrods in London was displaying New York Cosmos merchandise in 2012, decades after the team folded. New York City, the Big Apple, a truly world-class city, is bigger than the Red Bulls. The Cosmos will be racing to get back into the highest level in American soccer and start to promote the brand again. David Beckham vaulted the LA Galaxy into a recognized global brand. The New York Cosmos will attempt to follow a similar path back into top soccer circles.

Freddy Adu

Americans know Fredua Koranteng Adu as a player who hasn't lived up to his incredible potential. However, the jury is still out on his career as he is still only twenty-four years old and could make an impact again.

Born in Ghana, Freddy immigrated to the US in 1997 when he was eight years old. His family settled in Maryland, and he played soccer for a private school in Potomac. Soon after, he appeared on the US radar, joined the US Olympic Development Program, and then played with the varying age levels of US Soccer on the international level.

Freddy has lived on the fringes of the collective worldwide football consciousness for ten years, thanks to his brilliance that shone through at the U-17 and U-20 World Cup. He remains the only player in the world to score a hat trick in both tournaments. More importantly, he is the only American player I regularly get asked about from casual football fans in Europe.

"America sure has a long way to go, but whatever happened to the Freddy kid?"

People remember Freddy. They remember an American teenager playing the game better than English, Spanish, or Brazilian teenagers at the time, and they took notice and filed him away in the back of their minds, waiting for Freddy to resurface on the international stage. People outside the United States seem to be expecting another Freddy type of player to emerge and sustain.

"An American playing at that level?"

"Didn't he get a million from Nike when he was like fourteen?"

Fame, money, and the press in heavy doses are not easy for most adults to handle, let alone a fourteen-year-old boy. Freddy's professional career has seen him bounce around the world, playing for clubs in Turkey, Spain, Monaco, Brazil, and the United States, and he is currently training with English Club Blackpool while looking for a contract and staying fit. I haven't given up on Freddy, and more importantly, he hasn't given up on himself.

David and Victoria Beckham

When Posh and Becks made the decision to move to America in 2007, Brand Beckham won big and so did soccer in the United

States. It's hard to overstate the global appeal and reach of David Beckham. He was—and is still—a global superstar. His decision to transfer to the LA Galaxy after playing for giants Manchester United and Real Madrid baffled European soccer elites.

If the New York Cosmos first broke the path for top-level foreign players to enter the United States, David Beckham paved it. While David sincerely wanted to promote soccer in a largely untapped (relative to Europe) market, he also was going to clean house. David and Victoria realized, through some earnest consulting, that promotions go a long way, and they could leverage sponsorship earnings and showcase football at the same time. David has been to Japan, China, and Africa, and just about everywhere he goes, screaming fans meet him. He has transcended the game, and soccer fans in America should be grateful.

Posh and Becks together make a marketing dream. They are darlings in front of the camera. Americans view them as quintessentially British: stylish, good at football, fashionable, debonair, and respectful.

David Beckham's impact on the game in America was immediate. Ticket sales, attendance, and interest rose dramatically at the LA Galaxy and throughout the league. It was a smashing success. David Beckham wasn't even a superstar striker, like Messi or Ronaldo, the kind of scoring machines Americans love. He was a patient, deadly accurate midfielder who was one of the best free (dead ball) kick takers in the history of the game. This gives me hope that Americans aren't as fickle about sports as previously thought. America, like the rest of the world, fell for the accent, the hair, and the brand.

Surprisingly, success on the field for the LA Galaxy with Beckham took longer than most anticipated. They finally won the MLS title in 2011 and repeated in 2012 before he moved on. He left America and the MLS to see out his career in France with Paris Saint-Germain.

He left the MLS in far better shape than when he found it. The league probably would still be surviving if Brand Beck's had not come, but he clearly helped elevate the status of the league in America and around the world.

He also helped pave the way for top-level European players to come to America. French international Thierry Henry has been playing with the New York Red Bulls since 2010 after a stellar career with Arsenal and FC Barcelona. Henry is scoring in almost half of his games with the Red Bulls, helping them win the Eastern Conference and the Supporters Shield.

Algeria

It's been covered already, but the goal against Algeria was a significant milestone for the sport in the United States. Included here is a brief interview of an American soccer fan who was at the match. It shows the significance of the game to the team but also to the fans. My family and I met Kelly on the flight from London to Genoa en route to a soccer match. Kelly was at the 2010 World Cup and watched the United States versus Algeria match.

Me: Kelly, when did you first become a football fan?

Kelly: I started as a soccer fan by playing while growing up and during my freshman year in high school. After a few years away from the sport, I decided to coach a youth team in AYSO (American Youth Soccer Organization). With that decision, I started my journey to become a football fan. My first USMNT match was a friendly at the CSU Fullerton stadium with my nephew. I started watching the Galaxy regularly and even attended a football match in São Paulo in 2004. My first USMNT versus Mexico cap was earned when I attended the World Cup Qualifier in Columbus, Ohio, in 2005. It was my first true experience as a USMNT fan. Ever since then, I crave the excitement of watching the USMNT play. I attended the 2006 World Cup in Germany with my brother and friend. It was just the beginning. I now have a bucket list of games I want to attend, which includes the Champions League Final, World Cup Final, Euro Final, and so forth.

Me: What is your best football memory?

Kelly: My best football memory was the USMNT versus Algeria in South Africa. The game was a must win. We had a good number of opportunities but were unable to score. And Algeria got way too close to ending our dreams of moving on in the 2010 tournament. I remember commenting to my brother that it seemed like (Landon) Donovan was playing conservative and wasn't taking to their defense, which is his strength. I felt like it was in the coach's (Bob Bradley's) game plan, and it was hurting us. Then toward the end of the game, Timmy Howard distributed the ball to Donovan, and he actually took it down the wing. That attack didn't work, but I commented to my brother that Landon was finally doing what he should have all game. Then the magic happened. Timmy quickly released the ball halfway down the field to a streaking Donovan. He passed wide to Jozy, who crossed to Dempsey that sent the ball toward goal. The goalie blocked the shot with the ball trickling in front of goal, and here comes the hero, Landon Donovan, to the rescue. He scores! It was the best moment of my life. Yes, my life! (Especially since I'm not married and don't have kids.) The USMNT supporter section went wild in celebration—jumping, laughing, and screaming. Then after a minute of counting down, the triple whistle sounded, and celebrating happened all over again with new vigor. The players and fans celebrated in the stands for thirty minutes after the end of the best ninety-two minutes we've ever experienced. The trip was the best vacation I've even taken for so many reasons: new friends, safari amazement, best game of my life, and so forth. I will never forget and will be a fan for life. I will keep trying to replicate that feeling of pure joy.

That is the reason I made the trip to Brazil in 2014, to follow the team and try and replicate that moment of pure joy a national team can provide. A March Madness championship will never reach or have the same impact as Michael Phelps, Carl Lewis, or the 1980 US National Hockey Team. People will remember who scored that goal in the 2010 World Cup against Algeria.

Ghana

Sadly, the next match for the USMNT after beating Algeria in 2010 was Ghana. Ghana has a population of about 25 million.

If you combine Illinois and Pennsylvania, the resulting population and size are roughly the same as Ghana. Exports include gold, crude and refined petroleum products, electronics, rubber, wood, and world-class football talent. Ghana's U-20 and U-17 teams have won the FIFA World Cup of their respective ages. Ghanaian players suit up in all of the top leagues of Europe, playing at Italian clubs AC Milan, Juventus, and German side Schalke 94. They are a formidable opponent on the pitch, and they have enjoyed success on the global level. Of all the countries in the world, the football fates have put Ghana and the United States on collision courses in recent World Cups.

The Black Stars versus the Stars and Strips saga started in 2006 with Ghana hoping to make a statement in their first trip to the World Cup Final. Along with the United States, the group contained powerhouse Italy and the Czech Republic. Ghana and the United States each lost their opening games: the Czechs drubbed the United States 3–0 and Italy set back Ghana 2–0. Ghana won their second match against the Czechs while the United States produced a stirring effort to draw Italy. That second game of the group for Italy and the United States produced three red cards, one for the eventual champions and two for the United States, all in the first fifty minutes of the game. Playing for forty-plus minutes with nine men against Italy's ten, we survived with a draw to take a crucial point, which kept us in contention to advance.

In the final group matches, so long as Italy beat the Czechs and we beat Ghana, we would advance through with four points. Italy did their part, but we lost to Ghana, which eliminated any hope we had to advance from the group.

Looking back on the 2006 World Cup, the only blemish for Italy was the 1–1 draw. Several weeks later, Italy walked away as World

Cup champions for the fourth time, and the United States was left wondering how a World Cup debutante could have knocked us out.

In 2010, we advanced out of Group C as the top seed, meaning we would face the number-two seed from Group D. England finished second in our group, and it was paired with Group D winners, Germany. Ghana finished second, which meant Ghana stood in our way for the second straight World Cup. And again, we failed. Or Ghana prevailed. Ghana scored in extra time in a game that the United States was always playing catch-up. Our only goal was from a penalty that fittingly clanged off the inside of the post and in. The 2–1 loss ended 2010 World Cup dreams.

2014 saw the United States and Ghana group again along with eventual winners Germany and Portugal. Finally we vanquished Ghana in dramatic fashion. Finally we got the win we needed against our nemesis.

The Hiring of Jurgen Klinsmann

When Sunil Gualti, the president of US Soccer, announced the hiring of Jurgen Klinsmann as head of the USMNT, it was the beginning of a new era. Bob Bradley, an American, did a fantastic job, and he was the right coach at the right time. Under Bradley's guidance, the USMNT beat Spain in the Confederations Cup semifinals in 2009 and topped the group in the 2010 World Cup. Both of these were new highs for the team, but it was time to take the game to the next level. For this to happen, we had to look at a non-American, someone with the respect of the global football world, someone with an incredible playing career, someone who understands what will be needed to move the USMNT up the ladder of respect. (In a way, it is sad that an American isn't that person.)

Jurgen, the son of a baker, is extremely well known and respected in American soccer circles, but he is far better known in Europe and around the world. Jurgen had a Hollywood movie type career as a player, winning the World Cup with Germany in 1990. Jurgen now resides in California with his wife.

CHAPTER TWO

European Success: A Fan's Perspective

WHEN WE MOVED to London in mid-August 2011, I told my boys that, if either the USMNT or WNT came to Europe, we'd be seeing them in person, cheering them on and waving the Stars and Stripes. Shortly thereafter, the USMNT announced three friendlies on European soil against France, Slovenia, and Italy. This European tour featured two former World Cup winners and a team from our World Cup group in 2010. It was time for Dad to put up or shut up. We were joining the ranks of travelling away fans.

The USA-France game was on a cold November Friday night with a nine o'clock kickoff in Paris. My older son was running at a cross-country championship meet in Frankfurt on a Saturday morning, and he couldn't make the match as he needed to travel with his team from London to Frankfurt. I was determined to see the match and his meet. I am a parent and a fan. I purchased tickets to the USA-France friendly through the US Supporters group.

My younger son and I arrived at Stade de France to watch USA versus France men's teams at the site of the 1998 World Cup final, which France won. Over seventy thousand fans with what seemed like seventy thousand bleu, blanc, et rouge flags packed the stadium to cheer on Les Blues. Even though it was a friendly, the game was intense.

This game was a test for the players, but it was also one of the first main challenges for new head coach Jurgen Klinnsman as he balanced learning about his American players against playing an international friendly away against a top side. Howard, Dempsey, Altidore, Bradley, and Edu headlined the starters. We played well but gave up a goal off a long ball to substitute Remy in the seventy-second minute. Remy showed a flash of class and strength to shield the ball from the defender, and he then buried it. It would hold up as the game winner as we couldn't really mount much of an attack.

A 1–0 loss away to a European power is not a bad result, but a loss is a loss and doesn't move the respect barometer for America's game. We returned to our hotel, and to our surprise, the US broadcasting crew were discussing the game in the lobby. Even though it was almost midnight and they had just seen our boys lose, they were infectious with their enthusiasm for the team. We woke around four in the morning, hopped a flight to Frankfurt, rented a car, and made it in time to see the cross-country race. And it was a great race for Nicholas!

Then the USMNT beat Slovenia in Ljubljana on a cold, foggy night, which we did not attend. As far as I know, Koman Coulibaly did not attend. Nor did he referee the match, which saw the United States come away with a 3–2 win, an ironic score line considering we should have beat Slovenia 3–2 in the World Cup group stage in 2010. That game from 2010 featured an infamous disallowed goal that came from a Donovan free kick, which found Maurice Edu, who volleyed the ball into the back of the net. The referee blew the whistle and signaled no goal and nothing else. There was no call as to why he waved off the goal. Surprisingly, Koman didn't get another call to officiate any more matches that World Cup. This time though, we got the result against Slovenia on their turf, which brings us to the next friendly match on European soil.

Genoa, a beautiful city on the Mediterranean, is a great venue for a soccer match. The game was on a Tuesday night, which meant I had to pull the kids out of school for a couple days. I had some regret on the plane as I started thinking: am I going to win Poor Dad of the Year Award for pulling my kids out of school for a friendly football match? I'm glad that thought only lasted about three and a half seconds.

February 29, 2012, was that extra day stuffed into the year, a fitting day to see the USMNT get its first ever win over Italy, the four-time World Cup champions. It was also the only time that Italy has lost in Genoa. What a date to witness history. On the flight from London, my older son was sporting his Fulham FC Clint Dempsey jersey. A woman sitting directly behind us reached through the seats and tapped him on the shoulder.

"Are you going to the game?" she asked.

"Ummmmm, yes," we replied.

We has just met Kelly, the perfect American football fan. She had been to the World Cup in South Africa, and here she was on the flight from London to Genoa to watch the USA-Italy game. We'd see more of Kelly at the match inside Stadio Luigi Ferarris. We also saw more of Kelly over the next couple years in London as we would meet up for other matches.

We landed, found our hotel, and walked around Genoa as away supporters, not tourists. My three boys and I found a nice little Italian restaurant and had a fantastic meal while locals came and went with dogs and kids. Most folks gave us a double take as our style and look didn't quite mesh.

I imagined some of them thinking to themselves, *Americans here in Genoa for the match? The sport really has fallen to new lows.*

Everyone was friendly to us as we nourished our bodies with delicious local Italian food for a night of cheering.

We walked up to the stadium, purchased match day scarves from the street vendors, and showed our tickets a couple times to the stewards who pointed us to the visitor entrance. Once we found the correct entrance, we wandered around the large, secured area with a handful of other Americans, mostly military guys who came up from Camp Darby near Pisa. Many were partially intoxicated, but all were 100 percent supporting our team even if they weren't soccer fans. ESPN was there and filmed us jumping around, chanting "USA!" and waving flags. It was building.

Once inside the stadium, high above the supporters' section on the opposite side of the pitch, were hundreds of Italian schoolchildren singing and cheering. A battle ensued as they whistled and jeered to try to drown us out. More Americans came in. We mingled with the other red, white, and blue clad Americans. Someone brought face paint, and my kids got their faces painted in red, white, and blue. We had USA scarves, we had our voices, and we were ready.

After kickoff, wave after wave of Italian attack washed over the defense and keeper. Timmy Howard made many brilliant saves to keep the game scoreless. It was 0–0 at halftime. Whew, take a breather. The Italian players weren't nervous or anxious, but I sensed slight trepidation settling over the Italian fans. Surely they felt they should be doing better against the Americans.

With the second half underway, the Italians looked threatening again. They made run after run but just couldn't get the timing right with the high American defensive line as they were called for offside over and over. Now frustration was beginning to build for the Azzuri players. The United States finally got a break, and on the counterattack down the left side, deep into Italian territory, the ball was crossed to Alidore in the box, and he held himself up and played it perfectly to Dempsey, who steered the ball through two defenders and past a screened Buffon. The ball rolled over the line and up the back of the net.

I couldn't believe what we were seeing! We had a lead. We were playing soccer in Italy and winning! High-fiving, jumping, screaming, and hugging random fans, everyone was my best friend. It was USA 1–0 over Italy in the fifty-fifth minute.

Dread and doubt started to creep in as I fell victim to something I was fighting. Americans shouldn't win football matches against top European teams, especially away! I wiped away that thought and replaced it with belief. These Italian guys were just human beings. They got up in the morning and put on two socks, like the rest of us. We could hold them off for the remaining thirty-five minutes.

Doubt came back. Surely they'd tie it, and we'd be happy with that result. More than a half hour was an eternity. I told myself to calm down. We had a long time left with lots of work to do.

"Good, Carlos. A great professional foul. Don't let Pirlo do that. Look at Buffon's hair. I'm surprised his hair didn't make the save or even score a goal. Amazing, Howard. You are possessed. Seventy-five minutes. History? Eighty minutes. What? We are still winning! They've never lost a game in Genoa. Keep playing defense, boys!"

I looked around for my bleary-eyed, almost eight-year-old. He was standing toward the back of the pack of Americans with eyes transfixed on the pitch. Nicholas, I, and most of the other American fans were going crazy at this point. The green numbers on the sideline board indicating stoppage time went up: four minutes.

"Four minutes of time for what? Where was the referee crew from again?"

The adrenaline was pumping as we kept glancing at the ref.

"Blow the whistle already. C'mon! Ninety-four minutes and the final whistle! Yes! Yes! Yes! Yes! Amazing."

I didn't care if I were getting spit on or water was being dumped from above. We had just beat Italy on Italian soil.

The final and fitting clapping chant of the evening was just "Timmy Howard." He made amazing saves and looked determined to hold on to the win. We need just that type of steely determination in future World Cups.

There were only a few choice words from Italian fans in English as we left the stadium. I think we flew or floated back to the hotel with our new friend Kelly and agreed to meet up in London the following week for a recap. We were hungry, but this was Genoa, not London or NYC at eleven thirty at night, so we—just the kids and me—went to our hotel and celebrated without food. We were hungry for more.

The morning papers had to save a little face for Italy as one of the pages had a full color map of the United States showing some of the MLS teams. The headline read: "La Neuvo Frontier de Futbol." We moved the respect meter a little more with that result.

When we landed at Gatwick the next day, we were still high. It wasn't a dream. My older son was blowing the vuvuzela out the window of the car on the way home. David Geuta's "Titanium" came on the radio, and we blasted it. If books could have a soundtrack to tie the emotions of the writer and reader, this would be it. Every time I hear that song, I am reminded of Genoa.

We returned from Italy with an even stronger passion in our belly. My wife thought we were literally on drugs as we were still floating two days later. The friendly against Italy in Genoa on February 29, 2012, produced some real feelings of joy and dreamlike moments for my family.

"What are you giggling about?"

"The game! We beat Italy away. They hadn't lost in Genoa in two thousand years."

"Still?"

"Yes!"

All three hundred or so Americans at Stadio Luigi Ferarris in Genoa witnessed history. And we were going ballistic. That's the feeling multiplied by a hundred when America wins the World Cup.

And together we can dream of the day the USMNT gets the swagger of a Brazil team, the attitude of a Spanish side, or the arrogance of Bob Costas and brings the most coveted trophy in the world to America.

PART 2

CHAPTER THREE

Where We Are

O N THE VERGE of World Cup 2014, the United States was in tune with the game like never before. In April 2013, NBC announced a television deal with the English Premier League to make every game available in the United States.[11] NBC launched an ad campaign starring Jason Sudeikis as the phony American head coach of Tottenham Hotspurs, decorated some of the NYC subway system, and took over Times Square. Bring on the Barclay's Premier League in the USA.

Our top domestic league, the MLS, is gathering momentum. From 2012 to 2013, just about every MLS club increased attendance. Some stadiums are already at capacity. Only struggling LA-based Chivas USA saw notable declines in attendance. When Clint Dempsey made his debut for the Seattle Sounders in 2013, over sixty-seven thousand people turned up to CenturyLink field to see him play.

At the same time, significant strides were being made in the USMNT camp. Another pivotal moment in US Soccer history began in the summer of 2013 as the USMNT pushed its game to new levels under head coach Jurgen Klinsmann. It started with a friendly win over Germany in the centennial celebration game (one

---

[11]   www.si.com on April 16, 2013

hundred years of US Soccer from 1913–2013), followed by three extremely important WCQ wins over our regional competition.

Then the United States ran amok through the CONCACAF Gold Cup tournament, winning every game and dominating possession in the final with a 1–0 win over Panama. Yes, the US Gold Cup team was a B+ team of Americans trying to earn their way onto (or back onto) the A team, but these guys were unstoppable and showed the depth of the modern American team.

Next up saw USMNT travel to Sarajevo to play World Cup-bound Bosnia-Herzegovina, ranked thirteenth in the world at the time, in a friendly match without Landon Donovan and Clint Dempsey. We were down 2–0 at halftime and stormed out in the second half, scoring four straight goals. Edin Dzeko of Manchester City scored the final consolation goal of the match for Bosnia-Herzegovina to make it a 4–3 final. Jozy Altidore's second half hat trick and helper on the fourth American goal, combined with Michael Bradley's excellent midfield possession and distribution, were enough to not only win again in Europe but come from behind after being down. It was a friendly, but what European team wants to lose a home game to the United States? It was the twelfth straight win in all competition for the USMNT, a record.

We finally dropped a match away to Costa Rica during WCQ before wrapping up our home WCQs, beating Mexico and Jamaica each 2–0. Winning your home games is paramount to qualifying for the World Cup. Not only did the USMNT win every game at home in the final Hexagonal round, they didn't give up a single goal on American soil. That is an amazing run against any competition.

Having already secured our World Cup 2014 berth, our final match in WCQ took us to Panama, a team still hoping and praying for the fourth spot in CONCACAF that would earn a home and away, winner-gets-a-trip-to-Brazil series with New Zealand. It would be either Panama or Mexico in the fourth spot. Panama needed to beat the USMNT and have Mexico lose on the road to Costa Rica, another team that didn't lose a home match. Mexico was losing at Costa Rica, and Panama was winning. The games were being played simultaneously, and as they went into stoppage time, Panama was celebrating. They were winning 2–1 over the USMNT. We were resting Dempsey, Donovan, Bradley, and Howard with a mostly B team fighting it out on the road.

These players were fighting for a spot on the World Cup team. They were fighting to prove their worth to the coach. And they delivered. They delivered for themselves, they delivered for the respect of the USMNT game, and they delivered for Mexico. We scored two goals in stoppage time, breaking Panama's heart and sending Mexico, despite the loss to Costa Rica, into the playoff with New Zealand. Who says soccer is boring? Graham Zusi scored the first goal in stoppage time, which made it 2–2. That goal effectively ended Panama's World Cup dreams as they needed the win and all three points from the game.

Zusi is now a saint in Mexico as he and the USMNT salvaged a dreadful Mexican WCQ campaign. We bailed out our archrival, and Mexico was able to limp into the regional playoff against New Zealand. It was the Red Sox helping the Yankees sneak into the playoffs. Actually, it was much bigger than that.

		Score			Competition
W	USA	4	3	Germany	Friendly
W	USA	2	1	Jamaica	WCQ
W	USA	2	0	Panama	WCQ
W	USA	1	0	Honduras	WCQ
W	USA	6	0	Guatemala	Gold Cup
W	USA	6	1	Belize	Gold Cup

W	USA	4	1	Cuba	Gold Cup
W	USA	1	0	Costa Rica	Gold Cup
W	USA	5	1	El Salvador	Gold Cup
W	USA	3	1	Honduras	Gold Cup
W	USA	1	0	Panama	Gold Cup Final
W	USA	4	3	Bosnia-Herz	Friendly
L	USA	1	3	Costa Rica	WCQ
W	USA	2	0	Mexico	WCQ
W	USA	2	0	Jamaica	WCQ
W	USA	3	2	Panama	WCQ
T	USA	0	0	Scotland	Friendly
L	USA	0	1	Austria	Friendly

Figure 1. June, July, August, September, October, and November 2013 USMNT games. All competitions.

CHAPTER FOUR

US Women's National Team or USWNT

T HE AMERICAN WOMEN have tasted success at the highest levels of soccer. The USWMT has won the World Cup and Olympic gold medal multiple times. America leads the world in women's athletics, and it has developed youth and collegiate programs for girls and women to advance their skill. America has produced world-class players in just about every sport. However in soccer, one name in particular stands out.

Mia Hamm is synonymous with soccer in America. Her career is truly remarkable and inspired a generation of both sexes to play soccer. She was one of the most influential American athletes in the last thirty years and made commercials with Michael Jordan before becoming a football ambassador for FC Barcelona. In her playing days at the University of North Carolina, Mia won four NCAA titles. North Carolina lost one match in ninety-five when she played. She sat out the 1991 collegiate season to participate in the inaugural Women's World Cup. China hosted the tournament, which featured twelve teams that the United States won, beating Norway in the final. While Michelle Akers did most of the goal scoring, Mia at the age of nineteen was rock solid on the team.

It was just the beginning for Mia as she went on to score 158 goals for the United States, winning an Olympic gold medal as well. She simply played the game at a higher level than any other woman at the time. She was tenacious, patient, and skillful. She didn't have to chase the game; nor did she have to let it come to her. She existed within each game. Her touches and runs showed the brilliance of her vision. If you never got to see her play, please go to YouTube and watch.

The first Women's World Cup was a success. It was romantic and fun. Many of the women weren't professionals, that is, they had to take time off from their real jobs to train and compete for their country. Aside from the already mentioned teams, Italy, Sweden, Denmark, Chinese Taipei, Germany, Nigeria, Brazil, Japan, and New Zealand brought teams to China to compete. Every confederation was represented. It harkens back to the early days of the men's game with players who had day jobs and only moonlighted as footballers. They played for the love of the sport, not the fame or money.

In subsequent years, the Women's World Cup tournament grew to sixteen teams, and in 2015, Canada is slated to host twenty-four teams. I find it amazing that the first Women's World Cup wasn't until 1991. At least it's established itself now. The USWMT has only ever finished in the top three, having won twice, finishing as runner-up to Japan once in 2011, and taking third three times.

The second World Cup win for the US ladies was in 1999 and featured a penalty shootout which followed ninety minutes of regular time football and another thirty minutes of extra time football between China and the United States that produced no goals. China won the toss, elected to take the first penalty kick, and scored. Students of sports psychology and statistics will tell you that just by winning the toss and electing to shoot first gives you a significant edge. And they are right. (But that still doesn't explain

Germany's success or England's failure in PK competitions. Some studies suggest cultural differences may have a part to play.)

On that sunny day in the Rose Bowl from Pasadena, none of that mattered. Mia Hamm scored the fourth and penultimate US penalty, setting up Brandi Chastain to take the fifth, and if she made it, winning shot. It's one of my favorite YouTube videos. I can't image the pressure. One kick to win the World Cup. Brandi made it look easy.

Brandi walked up and placed the ball on the penalty spot. Confident and calm, she turned and walked back about five steps, not nearly as far back as some. She stood, calmly ran her hands over her hair, and kicked her toes on the ground as she inched closer to the ball. Koman Coulibaly blew the whistle, signifying she could shoot, and Brandi didn't hesitate. The Chinese keeper had no chance. Brandi hammered the ball to the right side of the goal, well off the ground. What transpired next helped catapult the game to new levels. Brandi took off her jersey, waved it over her head, dropped to her knees, raised her arms over her head, and flexed every muscle in her body in celebration. What a fitting response. Brandi will forever be remembered for scoring the winning penalty to win the World Cup for the USWNT.

As successful as the USWNT is, surprisingly, the women don't have a stable league in the United States although the National Women's Soccer League (NWSL) wrapped up the inaugural season with full expectations that all eight teams would return in 2014. This new league is connected to US Soccer, and many of the teams are associated with local MLS teams for support. The Portland Thorns won the title and drew crowds averaging over thirteen thousand as the Pacific Northwest continues its love affair with professional soccer. Some of the biggest names in the world play in the league, including Alex Morgan, Hope Solo, and Megan Rapino.

In 2012, my family and I saw the USWMT win gold in the London 2012 Olympic Games 2–1 over Japan at Wembley Stadium. It was redemption for the ladies after losing to Japan in the World Cup Final the year before. The ladies lost on penalties, which was painful but not as bad as it would have been if we lost to Mexico. The United States didn't strike the penalties well, and Japan raised the cup and jumped up and down in the confetti. It was nice to see them celebrating after a devastating earthquake and subsequent Fukushima reactor meltdown.

Our soccer friend, Kelly, flew from LA to London as we secured tickets to both the men's and women's gold medal matches. For the women's final, it was almost Canada-Japan, which would have been fun, but then we wouldn't have been able to unleash our red, white, and blue avalanche and screaming on Wembley. Thankfully, Alex Morgan headed home in stoppage time, saving the USA-Canada semifinal game from being decided on penalties and putting the American women through to the final.

At the gold medal match, my oldest son and wife donned USA morphsuits. If you're not familiar with a morphsuit, think body Spanx. They were head to toe in red, white, and blue! You can even cover your face with the mesh for a truly outrageous look. My younger son and I put on our USA jerseys, painted our faces, and dyed our hair. My wife put on her morphsuit at her central London office, and we met up with her and took the train to Wembley. We were going to the match in style, representing. My kids were probably in a dozen or more Facebook updates as American, British, Japanese, Canadian, Brazilian, Dutch, and Polish fans all wanted pictures taken with them.

London was sincerely excited to be hosting the Olympics. The city was buzzing. People actually talked with you and made eye contact on the trains! The atmosphere was celebratory, truly global and friendly. We had received a few warnings from friends and family back home. They were concerned we would be too "American" or whatever that meant.

Fans at all Olympic venues were sporting their country colors, wigs, Super Mario or Scooby Doo costumes, or whatever they fancied, and we were fitting right in. It was the Olympics, and we were on our way, along with eighty thousand other fans, to the largest-ever attended women's football gold medal match! It was the energy of the Olympic Games and the beautiful game colliding in a colorful extravaganza.

The USWNT had a dream start to the game, going ahead in the eighth minute. The game was a real gem, back and forth with Japan hitting the crossbar twice. It was 1–0 at halftime. We scored again shortly into the second half from a superb individual effort from Carli Lloyd, her second on the night, which turned out to be the game winner as Japan scored less than ten minutes later, setting up a frantic final thirty minutes. Hope Solo made fantastic saves as she bailed out the sometimes shaky back line. On the final whistle, we were hugging and jumping. This wasn't a friendly, it came with golden hardware, and it was a little bit of redemption for the ladies.

We stayed and watched the celebrations and medal ceremony, complete with the national anthem and the American flag flying proudly. It was a great feeling. We watched the USWMT head coach Pia Sundhage go into the stands and celebrate. We stayed until security kicked us out. We met other fans, not just American, celebrating and enjoying the Olympic spirit. It is contagious. Until then, it was the best sporting event I've ever attended. And in America, the women soccer players are just as, if not more popular, than the men.

Lingering Chauvinists

Some Americans still call soccer a girl's game. This is wrong on so many levels. I'm not going to get into all of them here. Conversely, I see another point of view, equally wrong, from male-dominated societies and cultures.

"Women should not be playing the game."

This is blatant, and not often do you hear it uttered directly, you see this mentality underpinning comments on the air and usually more directly from people hiding behind online names and avatars:

"It probably has a lot to do with the fact that no one gives a s— about women's football."

"OMG, who the hell cares?"

I usually tell these chauvinists to go read *Lean In* by Sheryl Sandberg as a starting point of reference to "re-center" themselves, knowing that most of these people are hardwired to think that way, and change will need to happen generationally.

CHAPTER FIVE

The American Outlaws (AO)

T HE AMERICAN OUTLAWS (AO) have recently replaced
Sam's Army as the dominant force in supporting the US
national soccer teams. AO started in Lincoln, Nebraska,
the heartland and breadbasket of America. Lincoln isn't known
for soccer, but it's certainly known for American football and the
Nebraska Cornhuskers football team. Yet AO has grown to over 150
chapters around the country. The name itself, American Outlaws,
taps into the counterculture nature of being a soccer fan in a region
(and country) where soccer is, at best, the number-five sport.

What's with Our Name? [bold added by author]
Our name came about in 2 ways.

1. When we started bringing soccer fans together to watch
   soccer and travel to US games in Nebraska (not known for
   soccer), we were part of an outlier group of sports fans in a
   sea of American football, baseball, and NASCAR fans. We
   felt we were outlaws of the sports world, supporting a sport
   that most people didn't know much of or care about. But we
   soon found out that many cared and many knew, no matter
   the size of your town.

2. We decided to show that **we were sports outlaws**, but weren't small in numbers, by sporting what the old American wild-west outlaws wore, the bandanna. We wanted to show we are proud of being American and proud to be a soccer fan in America! It also makes for a site to see in the stands![12]

With a country as big and expansive as the United States, organization is a critical aspect to creating a unified culture of soccer fans. AO organizes travel to home and away matches around the world so the team has passionate fans in the stands no matter where they play.

Unlike many other national teams, the US teams don't have a home stadium. The English national team plays all significant home matches at Wembley Stadium. The US national teams play matches all over the vast expanse of the country. This isn't always a bad thing, but it does highlight the need for broad, nationwide grassroots support no matter where the teams turn up to play or train.

The more the fan base is unified and the greater the fan presence, the more passionate the atmosphere. All will lead to better results on the field and growth of support of soccer. This is the goal of American Outlaws, to unite and strengthen.

The American Outlaws themselves have momentum, and they are growing. They will be key in providing coordinated support for the US national teams in the future for both home and away matches, including the World Cup. For the 2014 World Cup, they chartered flights to and around Brazil to celebrate and watch the Stars and Stripes.

Join AO and get to a game. Cheer on the red, white, and blue. They have harnessed the can-do American spirit, wrapped it in

---

[12]   www.americanoutlaws.com/about

patriotism and passion, and directed that energy at supporting the national teams. They are passionate, boisterous, and committed, and I love it.

They have several chants, and one of my favorites is based in the confidence that we can play with and beat any team in the world: "I believe that we will win."

CHAPTER SIX

Getting to the World Cup

Q UALIFYING FOR THE World Cup Tournament (also called the World Cup Finals) employs a variety of regional playoff systems, each long and grueling in its own right.

I was watching a Champions League match recently between Barcelona and Celtic. (Celtic hung on for a 2–1 win, shockingly.) Iniesta has caught my eye more than a couple times during the match. He seduces viewers and defenders, and he is a fantastic player who will be a national hero in Spain. Scoring the winning goal in the 2010 World Cup Final deep into the game will make anyone immortal: "Ladies and gentleman, this is the captain, we are beginning our descent into Iniesta International." Iniesta doesn't win popularity contests. He just commands the center of the pitch and sees lanes and passes that are sometimes lost on his own teammates.

Spain's success isn't limited to the top team. Watching the U 20 World Cup group game between USA and Spain in 2013 was not encouraging. We were outplayed on every level and looked cocky yet unable to live up to the skill our players thought they had. Spain plays with a lightness that comes from having fun. Having watched Spanish national teams of all ages and levels, you get the feeling that you could walk into a Spanish market and blindly select eleven apples. Those apples would be of a very high consistent quality and capable of beating any team. They are sweet, joyful, and refreshing, and produce World Cup glory.

Spain qualifies with ease as it continues to produce world class players, other countries have to battle, scrape, and claw to make the World Cup. Here is a look at the regions around the world and the qualifying process.

CONCACAF

In the CONCACAF, the pool starts as wide as possible with every country getting a chance to advance to the higher rounds. In the first round, only the lowest-ranked teams (according to FIFA world rankings) play such as St. Lucia and Aruba. In round two, more teams take part. Again, the next lowest-ranked teams compete. As the lower-ranked teams are knocked out, the highest-ranking teams are introduced until every country has played.

None of these teams competing in the early rounds generally survive to the sixth and final qualifying round call the Hexagonal or Hex. The Hex is competed amongst the surviving six teams, and they play for ultimate prize, a chance to compete in the World Cup Finals.

The Hex has a simple format. Each team plays every other team in the group twice, home and away. It's three points for a win, one for a tie, and none for a loss. The three teams at the top of the table after the dust settles automatically qualify for the World Cup. CONCACAF gets three slots for the World Cup, while the fourth-placed team plays a home and away series with the winner of Oceania for another World Cup spot, meaning Oceania gets only half a spot for the World Cup, unlike the Confederations Cup.

Dos a Cero

Dreams! Oh, heaven. We beat Mexico Dos a Cero again. Again! It was another magical result to secure all three points from Columbus, Ohio, in a WCQ 2013. This score line has become synonymous with the USA versus Mexico home qualifier for the USMNT. It's magic, pure bliss of ripping out the hearts of your archrival. We dispatched El Tri, sending them packing and thinking, "Will we ever beat the United States away?" Dos a Cero. If there were ever a case for someone to miss a penalty, it was for Deuce to boot the ball high in the ninety-third minute. Judging by the look on his face, he wanted to score it though, to do the 2–0 score line one better. Put Mexico's goal difference on notice.

In the end, it didn't matter. We took the lead 1–0 shortly after halftime off a leaping header from Eddie Johnson. He clearly showed why be belongs on the A team, if nothing else for his vertical ability. He nearly scored off a similar header earlier in the match, but Mexico's keeper and captain, Jose de Jesus Corona, made a brilliant save.

The second goal late into the second half came from a beautiful piece of skill from Mix Diskerud, working the ball around the Mexican defense and finding a streaking Deuce and Donovan. Donovan popped it into the roof of the net to set off the wild celebrations. We just punched our ticket to Brazil. Mexico was left reeling, wondering what was happening. They were supposed to be the dominant team from CONCACAF.

In all fairness, Mexico was in disarray, having fired their manager three days before the United States match after El Tri dropped a home game to Honduras and slumped to fourth place in the Hex. Mexico couldn't seem to win at home in the World Cup campaign, posting several draws, including a 0–0 result against America. It was a long slide for Mexico from 2012. Mexico was the talk of the football world when they beat Brazil to win Olympic gold in 2012. And it was a Brazil team that had Hulk and Neymar. It wasn't a walk in the park for them. Mexico scored right after the kickoff, and Brazil was reeling.

Since then, Mexico's MNT had been in a free fall, including that first ever home friendly loss to the United States. Mexico did qualify for the 2014 World Cup, and were grouped again with the host nation, with the host nation, along with Croatia and Cameroon. Brazil wanted to inflict revenge for the silver medal in London, but only managed a 0-0 draw. In 2010, Mexico faced a tough group with Uruguay and France in their group along with South Africa. France crashed out with only one point and finished the dreadful campaign with a loss to South Africa.

At risk of being disowned by American fans, I write the following paragraph. I love Mexico. I certainly love Mexican food. As an American soccer fan, I am supposed to cheer against Mexico in all contests, and for the most part, I do. But I also balance that rivalry against the broader campaign for respect. We are grouped with Mexico, Costa Rica, and Honduras geographically in the CONCACAF. And when they win big matches, like against Brazil in the Olympics, it makes the world raise their collective eyebrow a little higher. So only from that standpoint, I don't always find myself rooting against our regional peers. We do want CONCACAF teams to do well in international competition. I know. I know. They are the archenemy. But Europe views our region with an "over there" attitude, knowing that real football takes place in South America and Europe. And rightfully so, only South American and European teams have ever won the World Cup. And we don't have to qualify for the World Cup by flying around Europe or the real meat grinder that is CONMENBAL's qualification. How would you like that schedule: away to Brazil, home to Argentina and Uruguay, and then away to Chile and Paraguay. Yikes! At some point, a team not from Europe or South America will win the World Cup. Not Mexico, Ivory Coast, or Costa Rica, though. I want that to be the United States.

Oceania

The island nations of the Pacific get half a spot, meaning the team that finishes at the top of qualifying plays against a team from CONCACAF for a spot in the World Cup Final. This year, Mexico finished fourth and was paired up with New Zealand from Oceania. El Tri prevailed convincingly.

UEFA

European heavyweights such as Germany, Italy, Spain, and the rest of the fifty-three member nations are split into nine groups. For example, in this go-around of qualifying, Group E consisted of Switzerland, Norway, Albania, Iceland, Slovenia, and Cyprus, while Group A has Belgium, Croatia, Serbia, Macedonia, Wales, and Scotland. The teams in each group play each other home and away, and the team on top automatically qualifies for the World Cup. The eight best runners-up then compete in another round of competition, home and away, and the winners also qualify, kind of like a wild card in the States. At the end of the day, Europe gets thirteen spots for the World Cup. The nine outright group winners and the four runners-up qualifiers advance. This format produced a delightful match-up between Portugal and Sweden, two second place group finishers, which featured two of the best players in the world: Cristiano Ronaldo of Portugal and the imposing Zlatan Ibrahimovic of Sweden. Sadly, only one of these two would advance to play in the World Cup.

Africa

Africa's fifty-two teams compete for five spots. They narrow it down to ten teams, and then these teams are paired up and play a home and away with winner take all. Talk about an intense final qualifying round!

Asia

Four and a half spots are available for Asia. Australia, Japan, Iran, and the Korea Republic qualified. The half is Jordan, and they squared off against the fifth-place team from South America, Uruguay. Uruguay handily won and advanced.

CONMEBOL: Confederation Sudamericana de Futbol (Spanish), Confederacao Sul-Americana de Futebol (Portuguese)

Whatever you want to call it, South America gets four and a half spots. The World Cup host automatically qualify, not that they need it. The rest of the teams compete in one group for the remaining slots.

The 2014 Draw for Brazil

Once the thirty-two World Cup-bound teams are determined, the next process sorts the groupings for the tournament. This process is called "the draw." The draw is televised live all over the world from the host nation, and generally, the coaches of the teams are present as if being there would be helpful.

Before the draw, there is some jockeying to determine the pots or hats. So FIFA separates all thirty-two teams into pots. Each pot contains eight teams each and are generally divided out so top teams will avoid each other and countries from the same confederation will also avoid each other with the exception of European teams.

The current format for the World Cup group stage consists of eight groups of four teams. Each team plays three matches against their group opponents. One team is picked from each pot to determine the World Cup Final groupings. One team from pot four was drawn to go into pot two, Italy.

- Pot one contained the highest-ranked nations: Brazil, Spain, Argentina, Belgium, Colombia, Germany, Switzerland, and Uruguay. Switzerland? What?
- Pot two is the African teams and others: Ivory Coast, Ghana, Nigeria, Algeria, Cameroon, Chile, Ecuador, and Italy (from pot four). Surely we won't get Ghana in our group.
- Pot three is Asia and CONCACAF: Japan, Iran, South Korea, Australia, United States, Mexico, Costa Rica, and Honduras. Why do we have to be in this pot?
- Pot four is all the rest: Bosnia-Herzegovina, Croatia, England, Greece, Netherlands, Portugal, Russia, and France. This is a tough pot. And the United States got the highest-ranked team from this pot in its group.

The organizers avoid countries from the same confederation from playing in the same group with Europe being the exception. In the draw, the United States ended up with Germany, Ghana, and Portugal. If we look at the FIFA rankings at the time of the draw, this group is statistically the toughest.

Germany is ranked two, Portugal is five, the United States is fourteen, and Ghana is twenty-four for an average world ranking of eleven. The next closest is Group D with Uruguay, Costa Rica, England, and Italy with an average ranking of fourteen. The United States ended up with a very difficult group compared to 2010 when we had England, Slovenia, and Algeria. Okay, I've calmed down.

The online fallout from American fans during the selection was quite entertaining:

Sandy: Please give USMNT Group E!
Tara: OMG NOOOOOOOOOOOOOOOOOOO!
Roberto: That's awful. Germany and Ghana.
Roberto: Worst possible draw.
Marcia: Fuuuuhhhhhh!
Richard: Ouch.
Sandy: I'm going to teach Omar (Gonzolez) how to take out Chirstiano!
Tarih: Oof!
Gerry: And Portugal? Take it easy on us, Ronaldo.

I have a little disclaimer about the FIFA Coca-Cola world rankings. Brazil automatically qualifies for the tournament as hosts and doesn't play in WCQ. As the other countries play qualifiers, it boosts their standings on the official FIFA rankings table relative to Brazil. Also, Portugal (and other European teams that finished second in their qualifying group) had to play two extra matches against a tough Swedish team so their ranking gets boosted a little. That is, if you took an informal survey, many wouldn't put Brazil at number ten or Portugal at number five, but perhaps switch them.

Breaking Our World Cup Pattern

We finally broke it. In 1990, we exited the World Cup in the group stage. In 1994, we left in round of sixteen. In 1998, again, it was the group stage. In 2002, we shocked the world and made it to the quarterfinals. In 2006, it was a group stage exit, and of course, we all know what happened in 2010. 2014 saw us survive the Group of Death only to run into Belgium. We gave them a mighty battle and even had a chance to win late in the game. Surely Landon Donovan would have buried it. It was a heartbreaking end to our dreams.

But what if we are dreadful in a future World Cup? Has the sport come far enough for the fan base to endure a painful early World Cup exit? It will happen again. It happens to the best teams. Look at France in 2010. They were champions of the world in 1998 to crashing out of the 2010 World Cup, winning none and only scoring one goal in three matches. Italy, like France, finished bottom of its group in South Africa that included powerhouses New Zealand and Slovakia. Anything can happen.

I do think the sport has moved on enough in America. People will feel it if we crash out, and it will hurt. And that is a good thing. It's not always going to be Hollywood-type drama with Algeria. It will sometimes be like the 4-0 whooping Spain put on the United States in 2011. We were at home, a little Spanish payback for the 2009 Confederations Cup.

The revamped US Soccer supporters club and the surge of the American Outlaws will continue to drive the increased organization of US fans to matches, pubs, and gathering spots.

The Three Lions

England were in a group with Italy, Uruguay and Costa Rica. Another very difficult situation. Los Ticos were the only team in the group that hasn't won a World Cup but they defended well and surprisingly finished top of the group. They represented CONCACAF well while leaving England to wonder what might have been.

While we are on the subject of England, their governing body is simply the FA. It doesn't need to be called anything else as it was the first football association in the world. This is the governing body of football in England, and it is the grandfather of all things pertaining to the organized game. FIFA looks to the FA for guidance. The FA organized the first Cup competition in 1871, and fifteen teams competed. Today, more than seven hundred teams compete for the FA Cup.

Most other countries have a similar "cup" for the top club team, separate from the league. In America, this is the US Open Cup, also called the Lamar Hunt US Open Cup. Some competitions allow for upstart teams to compete above their level, like the open cups. Sometimes competitions will even allow for an upstart country to play well above its level.

The Confederations Cup

The Confederations Cup is a World Cup warm-up tournament played a year ahead of the World Cup in the host country. In 2009, South Africa hosted a great Confederations Cup, which Brazil won over a surprising United States 3–2 in the final. (And the United States was leading 2–0 at halftime!) Brazil hosted and won the 2013 edition of the Confederations Cup in June in preparation for 2014. Brazil played great football and dismantled Spain 3–0 in the final, allowing Brazilian fans to forget the silver medal they took home from the Olympics at the hands of Mexico. But the Cinderella story at the 2013 Confederations Cup was Tahiti!

Naysayers in the media think allowing teams like Tahiti in playing detracts from the sport. Rubbish! If you play the game in true spirit with love of the game and respect for your opponent, it can only be good for the game. It is just like a sixteen versus one seed in the NCAA basketball tournament. No sixteen seed has ever won, but they still play the game, and the sixteen seeds are thrilled just to be playing.

Tahiti qualified for the Confederations Cup as champions of the Oceania Football Confederation, along with other regional champs, Mexico, Nigeria, Uruguay, and Japan. Tahiti didn't put up much of a fight to any of the teams, as they lost to Spain and Uruguay by a combined 18–0. Tahiti also lost to Nigeria but managed to score a goal, dropping the game 6–1. But the tears on the faces of the Tahitian players at the final whistle of their final game, the storylines, and the respect of the game made it emotional and fun and highlighted what is right about soccer in the world.

Aside from the regional champs, Brazil qualified as hosts of the World Cup, and Spain qualified as current world champions. Because Spain also won UEFA's championship over Italy, the Italians qualified from UEFA, so it can be a little give-and-take:

Teams in the 2013 Confederations Cup

Mexico	Champions of CONCACAF (The Gold Cup)
Nigeria	Champions of CAF - Confederation of African Football
Uruguay	Champions of CONMEBOL (Copa America)
Japan	Champions of AFC - Asia Football Confederation
Tahiti	Champions of OFC - Oceania Football Confederation
Italy	Qualified as UEFA Runners-up
Spain	Reigning World Cup and UEFA Champions
Brazil	Qualified as Hosts

The CONCACAF just changed its format for qualifying for the next Confederations Cup. The United States won the 2013 Gold Cup, the trophy awarded the CONCACAF champion, but because the Gold Cup is awarded every two years and the Confederations Cup only every four, the winner of the 2015 edition of the Gold Cup will play the United States for a spot in the next Confederations Cup. Get it? Good. If the United States wins the 2015 edition of the Gold

Cup, the United States will automatically represent CONCACAF in the next Confederations Cup.

The Olympics and Soccer

The Olympics and soccer have a tricky relationship. It is an important competition, but due to some grand agreement between FIFA and the Olympics, each country can only have three players over the age of twenty-three on their Olympic soccer team. So it isn't always top quality, which is what FIFA wants. Nonetheless, the final between Mexico and Brazil in London 2012 was a hard-fought contest, and Brazil was visibly distraught after the loss. They brought a very good team that included star players Neymar and Hulk. Mexico scored just after the opening kick and never looked back. When it was all settled in London, it was gold for Mexico, silver for Brazil, and bronze for South Korea.

CHAPTER SEVEN

Love the Game; Love It Not

THERE ARE MANY misconceptions about why more people in the United States don't follow soccer. I will summarize some of my findings here. Reasons like not enough scoring or the proliferation of hooliganism are worthy discussions to have in the context of the modern game. Are they still relevant? The first two reasons—not enough scoring and the nil-nil draw—are related.

Reason #1: Not Enough Scoring

Many comments I've received from English and Europeans were around the same generalizations of impatient Americans. The rest of the world thinks we don't have the attention span to watch a 0–0 game. Maybe that is a valid point. American football and basketball have plenty of scoring. Like NBC's phony Tottenham Hotspurs coach Ted Lasso (played by Jason Sudeikis) says when told that some matches end it in ties, "If you tried to end a game in a tie in the United States, heck, that might be listed in Revelations as the cause for the apocalypse... Ties and no playoffs, why even do this?"[13]

But baseball doesn't end in ties, Bud Selig's 2002 All-Star Game disaster aside. But if Americans have patience for baseball, surely we have the patience and fortitude for a scoreless soccer match. I know

---

[13] http://metro.co.uk/2013/08/04/spurs-appoint-new-american-football-coach-jason-sudeikis-sort-of-3910972/

that the top billing on baseball highlights is usually home runs. But baseball scoring does hinge on a few crucial plays with buildup and release, exactly like soccer. A pitcher's duel can be like a low-scoring soccer game. A closer shutting down the three, four, and five hitters in order in the ninth inning is like a goalie making clutch saves in the waning moments of the game.

The only time I've seen the New York Yankees play in person was a 1–0 pitcher's duel with the winning run coming in the bottom of the ninth inning, a walk-off home run, just like a goal being scored in extra time. Instead of a walk-off, in soccer, it's "last kick."

American respect for the game is growing along with our understanding. This is one reason that can be overcome in time if it isn't already. The score doesn't need to change all the time to keep Americans interested.

Another example of this is a 1–0 victory. One goal was the margin of victory for the USMNT over Algeria. That was the best of a 1–0 win. The worst is a similar score line determined by a marginal penalty. An inadvertent handball that probably wouldn't have led to a goal in the first place can magically award a victory and all three points to a team. What if it were a high stakes match?

During a knockout game in the World Cup into extra time, we see an unintentional handball near the corner of the box on a pass leaving the box out to another player. Should that decide the match? Later in the book, I mention Luis Suarez's intentional handball to keep the ball out of the back of the net. Of course, that deserved a penalty and subsequent red card, but the handball call is rarely that clear-cut.

Sometimes a tie and the point that comes with it can be just as good as a win. The USMNT 2010 World Cup match against Slovenia had that feel. We were down 2–0 with hopes of advancing from the group quickly fading away. Thankfully, Landon Donovan willed a goal on his own to bring the United States back. Michael Bradley then karate-kicked in the tying goal, sparking celebrations from the team and country. (Yes, we also scored a third but disallowed goal, but compared to the feeling at halftime, it still felt good.) And sometimes a draw can feel like a loss. The USA v Portugal 2-2 result in World Cup 2014 was very painful.

Reason #2: The Dreaded 0–0 Draw

In many of the unscientific surveys for this book, people were asked about scoring in the game or a lack of scoring as a deterrent to enjoying the game. One of my Irish relatives told me that the best match they ever saw was a 0–0 draw. He went on to explain the athletic saves, rapid counterattacks, and crisp passing. Okay, I wasn't totally sold, but I got his point. Soccer can be amazing and breathtaking even without the ball hitting the back of the net.

A 0–0 draw can feel like a loss, and it can feel like a win. Suppose the United States needed a draw to advance out of a group from the final game. A 0–0 draw against a top-ten team in the world would feel like a win. It can also feel like a loss. The USMNT played fifty-four games in calendar years 2011–2013, and four resulted in a nil-nil draw. Two were friendly matches against Canada that we should have won. We didn't bring our A game or A team to either match, and all matches involving Canada are really friendlies anyway. These were probably some of the worst results over that time as Canada is a team we should handily and regularly beat, even with our B team.

I do feel a little for Canada, though. They were close to making it to the CONCACAF Hex for the 2014 WCQ. They were playing well, having beat Cuba and Panama along the way. In their final match against Honduras in the group stage, all they needed was a draw to advance. Sadly, they were soundly picked apart 8–1 as the Canadians melted in the Honduran heat.

If it is any consolation for Canada, the better team beat them as Honduras did advance on to the Hex and then punched a ticket to the FIFA World Cup in Brazil, finishing clear of Mexico by four points. Another of the 0–0 draws was a WCQ against Mexico in Mexico City.

Getting a point on the road in WCQ is huge, and it shouldn't matter if the game is 3–3 or 0–0, and if it's against Mexico, it is like a win. The usually stingy confines of Estadio Azteca yielded a few times in 2013 and relinquished points to CONCACAF teams.

In that match, we had to absorb a ferocious Mexican attack, and in all honesty, Javier Hernandez was unlucky. (And I despise the overused term, but it is appropriate in this situation.) Our number-two keeper, Brad Guzan (of Premier League side Aston Villa) made brilliant saves, and we came away from Estadio Azteca with a point. Yes, Mexico wasn't playing well and had dropped points at home to other teams during their road to Brazil, but celebration from the USMNT showed the significance of the result. Nonetheless, again it was history being made in the Klinnsman era.

The other 0–0 draw was the friendly against Scotland in Glasgow.

Glasgow and Change

On Friday, November 15, 2013, the USMNT played its first friendly game since qualifying for the World Cup. It was against Scotland in Glasgow, and again, my boys had to miss a day of school to see the match. We almost didn't make it to London's Stanstead airport as a truck overturned on the highway, spilling its load of steel cables. If we missed the flight, we would have taken to the highway: London to Glasgow. We weren't going to miss the match. Backup plans were formulating in my mind as we were navigating through the county roads. Drive all day? Hitchhike? Or try to catch another flight? We parked the car, sprinted through the terminal, and made it to the gate well past the cut-off time printed on our boarding passes. Thankfully easyJet kept the gate open, knowing the situation on the highway.

Once in Glasgow, it was time to make signs. We checked into our hotel and headed straight for the nearest High Street office supply store. We settled on "We are going to Brazil" and "You're Welcome, Mexico." We purchased tape, glue, poster board, and markers. Mission accomplished. It was off to the pub to engage fans.

The unofficial European chapter of the American Outlaws organized a meet-greet-and-drink-heavily in a pub about a five-minute walk from Hampden Park, the venue for the match. Unfortunately, kids were not allowed in, so my two boys and I ventured down the road to another pub with slightly relaxed rules that allowed children. We mingled with Scots in kilts, had our pictures taken, and chatted nicely with Scottish families prepping for the match as well. My older son dug out his USA morphsuit and wore that to the pub and match.

The Scottish are very friendly, and Glaswegians are some of the nicest around. Sadly for them, their team did not qualify for the World Cup. They were in a group with Belgium, Croatia, Serbia, Wales, and Macedonia. Belgium won the group, and Croatia, a team Scotland beat twice, finished second and then qualified through the UEFA playoffs against Iceland.

We walked back to the pub where the main group of Americans was gathered. I walked in just as they were all posing for a picture and held up the "You're Welcome, Mexico" sign. Chants of "Dos a Cero" erupted, followed by "Cinqo a Uno," a reference to the 5–1 thrashing the USMNT put on Scotland in Florida the previous year. Then there was a favorite of the night, "We are going to Brazil," followed by a smaller yet very vocal group of Americans that would carry on with "You're not going to Brazil."

With that last chant, we were deep in proper football territory and giving them the business. It was the only edgy part of the evening. Our walk up to the stadium was full of songs and flag waving. The Stars and Stripes was on display.

If we had thought of it, we should have incorporated Scotland's national animal into the banter. Surely, unicorn references would have made the night even more enjoyable because the game itself wasn't much to write about. We had our chances, and the play of Shea and Johansson were encouraging but obviously lacking on the final touch. It really was just a test for some of these guys, playing in the penultimate international match in Europe. The final result was earned by both sides, and at least the boys and I have another wonderful experience to treasure. My inbox had an email from my father after the final whistle that simply read: 0–0 WTF?

A pleasant surprise was having a young Scottish journalist take an interest in the American team and supporters. His name is Michael Temlett, and he was writing for www.theawayend.net. While he talked about going behind enemy lines to the pub where the unofficial European chapter of the America Outlaws were gathering, his journey and subsequent two-piece exposé of United States away supporters was fantastic even if it did have a tinge of what most American fans are used to seeing and hearing. "What do Yanks know about the sport?"

To be fair, Michael certainly helped the world understand that Yanks do know more about soccer than they think. Not that it was his mission, but we'll take any help we can get. From Michael's article, "The American Outlaws Showing the Potential of USA Soccer," "Many of us in this country (Scotland and UK) have claimed that, if Americans can't get the name of the sport right, will they ever truly understand football?" What was his answer after spending time with us? "The American Outlaws certainly do."

Michael was gracious and let me turn the tables. I added the bold emphasis.

> MK: Did your impression of US football and fans change?

> MT: Before, during, and after the match, I realized that, for the Americans that had made the trip across, they loved football. It sounds like a very bland thing to say, but I've witnessed big Champions League games, European Cup finals, and Old Firm (Rangers and Celtic) matches, and I didn't think it was possible for American fans to show as much passion for the game as I'd seen at the aforementioned games. It completely shocked me, but I was pleasantly surprised as it showed that you guys are taking football seriously, a criticism which was often made.

> MK: Did you cheer for the United States when we were in England's (World Cup) group in 2010?

> MT: I did cheer for the United States in 2010 because of the rivalry we have with England, but also because I thought that the USMNT was starting to take themselves seriously. I realize now, though, that they were only showing a glimpse into the potential that you have. With Jurgen Klinsmann at the helm, I think you have really

turned a corner. I'll definitely be supporting you in Brazil after talking to your fans and hearing of their excitement for next year.

MK: Can the MLS ever rival the top European Leagues?

MT: I think it is dependent on the next decade of the MLS history. With the expansion involving Orlando, NYCFC, and the rumored franchise in Miami being funded by Beckham, I think eventually Don Garber has to decide on a number that will make him happy. Too many teams risk diluting the quality, especially considering you have NASL teams waiting in the wings for a pyramid system. If the MLS decides in the next decade to stop adding teams and introduce a promotion and relegation scheme, then it will certainly be among the top-five leagues in the world. Most teams already have a loyal fan base, and as long as the fans continue to support their side, then the league can only improve.

MK: Can the USMNT ever win the World Cup?

MT: Ever is a long, long time! Yes, they can, maybe not in Brazil. Maybe not even in Russia and Qatar. But there will certainly be an improvement made at each tournament. I think it correlates with the MLS. The stronger that league becomes, the stronger the national team is. I also think it relies on factors outside of the United States, for example, a great footballing nation like Brazil or Spain may have to fall away to make room for the USMNT. But do I expect to see the United States win the World Cup in my lifetime? Absolutely.

Michael's deep answers about the MLS expansion surprised and encouraged me. Granted, anything Beckham touches is news around the world, but to reference the MLS commissioner when most Americans have no idea who he is is impressive and shows that the MLS is starting to crack into the global consciousness. Sometimes it feels that Europeans understand the MLS better than most Americans.

We didn't make the trip to Vienna, but the team ended the year with a rare loss, dropping to Austria 1–0. The final two matches of 2013 were anticlimactic for the record-setting year, but somehow fitting as those results allowed the team to reflect and look ahead to the looming job in 2014.

Reason #3: Rioting and Hooliganism

Concerns around safety are real and should not be taken lightly whether it's a crush of people at a match or someone falling from a balcony. People should be able to watch a sporting event without worrying about injury.

Rioting comes up often. Drunk fans and thugs beat on each other in the stands during and after the game, prowling the streets around the stadiums, and lurking in shadows. Sometimes we hear about riots breaking out. When it does happen now, it is usually from a lower league in a developing or Eastern European country. Or they are leftover ultras or nationalists with extreme right-wing agendas. The big clubs can afford hundreds of stewards and have a vested interest in promoting a safe setting for home and away fans.

I've been to many games and never felt threatened or in danger as a mass of stewards and security line the pitch to protect the players from the fans and more along the stairs, at doorways, and outside the stadiums to keep people calm. Mounted police also provide an intimidating and calming effect. Granted, these games are usually top level and can afford such luxuries. But considering all of the matches that take place in all the leagues around to world, rioting doesn't happen as often as Americans think it does. Perhaps it is still a lingering legacy from a darker time in the sport that hasn't been purged from America's perceptions.

Reason #4: Flopping, Diving, Simulation, and Acting

This is a valid point. Flopping is a problem and happens on a regular basis, and it happens in the States. Spain, Italy, and Portugal all have great traditions of flopping.

I took my boys to an MLS game and saw this firsthand. A player went down from a challenge, and he was rolling around the pitch on his back, holding his ankle and looking like a dying beetle when the ball rolled right to him. He popped up, suddenly healed. (The ball must have had healing powers.) Then he latched onto the ball and started running with it. The crowd collectively laughed at this sight even as it was their player. It is an issue, and some countries in Europe tend to flop more than others do. Sometimes it can be funny.

Didier Drogba was lying on the ground with his hands over his eyes, and the camera zoomed in on his face. He then peeked through his fingers with eyes smiling, looking to see if the ref was going to side with him. It is entertainment after all and gives the commentators something to talk about.

The worst of flopping happens when a player is trying to win a penalty. There are swan dives, arms and legs arched back, and a grimace on the face at even a hint of a challenge. At home on the couch or in the pub, we have the luxury of replays and can see the comedy in the beautiful game. On the pitch, when the ref sees it and it is blatant diving, players can get booked. And they should! The problem goes back to the high reward for a successfully executed swan dive in the penalty area. Now that goal-line technology has been implemented, tackling this problem should be next. Harsh, retroactive punishments for diving in the penalty area may help stamp out one of the major, justified criticisms of the sport.

Reason #5: Match Fixing

The promise of making a fortune playing your favorite game is alluring. When a player reaches a level just below the life-changing money and feels the career stalling, it can be frustrating and tempting to contemplate fixing a match as a way to supplement income. Maybe he just wasn't good enough to be a world-class player. Maybe the player lost the injury lottery. Maybe the cards didn't fall his way. Maybe he was just unlucky.

It's easy to see how players can turn to the lucrative world of match fixing as a source of supplemental income. The continued globalization of the game not only creates new fans but makes the football talent pool wider. If you combine that with the proliferation of betting in developed and developing nations, you have a Petri dish for international match fixing syndicates. In England, you occasionally hear about lower league players being associated with shady "Asian crime syndicates."

But is this a reason America shouldn't like the sport? Probably not. America has its own history of match fixing scandals, some quite famous. It hasn't degraded the sport, although one could argue Pete Rose did leave a black eye on baseball after he admitted to betting on teams he was managing, even if it were to win. People still watch and attend baseball games.

Reason #6: It's Not Our Game

"It's not our game... We don't need that sport played by foreigners." I don't really understand this argument, and I've heard it many times from Americans who don't support the sport. It isn't valid if people understand the historical context of the game in America.

And "foreigners." This word when uttered in a derogatory way by Americans makes me scratch my head. Unless we are Native American or Native Alaskan, aren't we all foreigners in the New World? Worse still, they think football is for kids who can't play American football or basketball.

It doesn't hold when applied to the only other truly global game that is played in America: basketball. Have you looked at an NBA team recently? Vlade Divac is retired, but a whole host of internationals, ninety-two to be exact at the tip-off of the current NBA season, have replaced him.[14] American fans embrace Manu Ginobili (Argentina), Tony Parker (France), Dirk Nowitzki (Germany), and Luol Deng (South Sudan via Great Britain), to name a handful.

Reasons Why Americans Should Love the Game

If you can't think of any, I'm going to spell it out for you in simple terms.

Reason #1: The Players

If you're a great player, you play for a club team and your country, and you employ your trade all over the world. Think David Beckham, Michael Bradley, Landon Donovan, and Thiery Henry. You play in your home country, and you play with your club, which

---

[14] www.nba.com/global/nba

may or may not be in your home country. And on the national team, you play in tournaments around the world.

Landon Donovan's goal against Algeria in the 2010 South African World Cup to secure the top spot in our group wasn't pretty. Perhaps the best piece of play on that scrappy workmanlike goal was Tim Howard's save and heads-up throw out. But it ended up in the back of the net, securing top place for the United States in the group. It is a candidate for a top, meaningful American goal. However, in my opinion, the best goal combining beauty and ability came from the previous year in the same country. The United States was winning 1–0 over the mighty Brazil in the first half of the 2009 Confederations Cup final in South Africa. Brazil was attacking on the right side, and they made an errant pass that the United States picked up. Landon Donovan showed his world-class ability with three touches. If you haven't ever seen the goal he scored against Brazil, it is certainly worth a look. His first touch played the ball long down the left side well into Brazil's half, and another counterattacking American met it. Brazil was scrambling back to cover, and the simple cross came in. Landon's second touch completely changed the direction of the play, and he had the defender looking over his back to try to make a turn. Landon's third touch put the ball into the net at the far post ahead of a sprawling keeper. It was sheer class, a beauty.

The point of bringing up this particular goal is that it showcases American talent at the highest level against the toughest competition. Our players can compete with anyone in the world. Donovan's goal against Brazil was patient, calm, and clinical. It was world class against the best.

Sometimes you have to tip your hat to the better opponent. Brazil took it to us in the second half. I remember watching the awards ceremony and the look on "Deuce" Clint Dempsey's face as he accepted his medal for second place. He was sad, pissed, and proud at the same time, knowing we let the game slip away. We let a tournament trophy slip away. It was that hunger to prove to America and the world that we are so close to the next level, ready to take the next step up. I love that about Deuce. He is a professional, and he is passionate about the game.

Get excited about our players. They are passionate and want to move the sport to new levels in the United States.

Reason #2: Sportsmanship

Baseball players, baseball advocates, and followers talk about the unwritten rules of the game of baseball. Some of these golden rules of baseball have roots in respect: respect for the other team, respect of your own teammates, and respect for the game and its history. The following rules are based on respecting the other team:

- Don't slow walk a home run trot, especially if your team is leading comfortably.
- Don't steal a base when your team is leading 9–0.
- Hit the home run, and run at a reasonable pace around the diamond. It's okay to high-five the first- and third-base coaches, touch home plate, and then trot back to the dugout.

Others have to do with the flow of the game.

- Don't bunt to break up a no-hitter late in the game.
- Don't step in front of the catcher on the way to the batter's box.

However, some of the rules are on the opposite end of sportsmanship and one in particular is a doozy. "If a pitch hits one of your players, your pitcher should retaliate." This rule is still carried out, and the merits of which will be forever debated on sports talk shows ad nauseum.

Soccer has generally very sportsmanlike unwritten rules, and one in particular can affect the flow of the game. The most notable unwritten rule in soccer occurs when a player is injured and the referee hasn't noticed or decided not to stop play. The team with the ball will play the ball out of bounds so the injured can receive medical attention. Once the injured player has been removed or attended to and reinstated to play, the team taking the throw in will deliberately play the ball back to the other team, usually back to the defense or keeper. When a player is injured and play continues, the crowd usually starts catcalls and whistles to express violation of this rule.

All in all, the players in football are very sportsmanlike. They shake hands and even swap jerseys after a match. There is the general sense that what occurs on the pitch, stays on the pitch. Isn't that what we are all taught as kids? Shake the other players' hands? I find it bizarre that the players shake the hands of their teammates after a MLB game. What is that all about? You need to congratulate yourselves?

Reason #3: The Players Are Extremely Fit and Athletic

When folks from America come to visit us in London, we usually take them to a Fulham FC match, and they are amazed at the athletic ability of the players. It's their first and, in most cases, only exposure to European football.

As with most professional athletes, soccer requires players to be extremely fit. Yes, of course you can find lists of "fat footballers" online, and it is funny to run through them, but in all honesty, it is one of the most physically demanding sports. American sports are built for more explosiveness, speed, and strength for short intervals with plenty of substitutions and timeouts. The beautiful game has no timeouts, and the defense really only gets to catch its breath when its team is attacking. And even then, some of the wide backs join in up the pitch while the central defenders hold the line, and sometimes they join in as well. The midfielders are in motion all the time and have superior fitness levels, sometimes logging between six to eight miles a game or more.

I'm not sure the sports drink commercial with the sweaty baseball players is realistic, except perhaps the pitcher. All in all, soccer players are the most fit.

Reason #4: Americans, Underdogs, and Patriots

America loves an underdog, and the USMNT are underdogs in the soccer world. It isn't surprising anymore. Shortly after the 2014 draw, many predicted the United States wouldn't get out of a very tough group. Perhaps. But these same people picked us to barely scratch out of the group in 2010, and we finished top.

Anyway, I put less stock in the media heads than the bookies. Unfortunately, the bookies dropped the USA from 100–1 to 150–1 odds to win the World Cup after the draw due to the tough group. Surely, the bookies are underestimating the can-do American spirit. We shocked the world and beat Portugal in our only other World Cup meeting with them, we beat Germany in a friendly in 2013. Unfortunately after our opening win over Ghana, we didn't win another match in Brazil. When we faced Germany in our final group match, we already had 4 points and were playing not to lose by three or four goals. We certainly didn't play to win. The celebrations were muted compared to 2010 because it didn't feel right. Not only does it seem un-American, but advancing on a loss doesn't really set the psyche in the right direction for the matches ahead. Yet Americans turned out in droves to watch USA v Belgium.

The USMNT is no longer a fringe team on the bubble of greatness, yet we are still an underdog to the top nations. It's a perfect combination. The passion people have for sport and country is amazing. We want to beat the world at its game and, in the process, make it our own.

Portugal is fantastically talented at some positions, but they are lacking a bit at other positions. Can their global superstar be enough? Looking at their qualifiers, they didn't set the world on fire with a tie at home against Israel and an away draw to Northern Ireland in Belfast. The best display of their WCQ campaign was when the Swedes had their back against the ropes and were pressing the attacks. Ronaldo feasted on the scant defensive fodder at the back scoring some memorable goals.

Reason #5: We Love Sport

When the United States hosted the 1994 World Cup, 3.59 million people attended fifty-two matches, the highest attendance on record even with recent World Cups expanding to sixty-four matches. It was record numbers of spectators in a country where soccer was maybe a number-five sport.

Reason #6 Our Home Matches?

I also love America and its diversity. Diversity is a strength of the United States for our economy and our culture. It's not a strength, though, when we play a home match in Los Angeles against Mexico. More fans turn out to cheer for Mexico. It's the same for matches against Panama or Costa Rica. This is partly because many people who are first- or second-generation Americans are extremely passionate about the sport and their home country. And that is a good thing on the whole, for the game in America, the MLS, and the growth of soccer culture in America. But it isn't always for the UNMNT home matches.

So we schedule matches away from the southern border in places like Denver, Seattle, and Columbus so we can have more fans cheering on America. After all, that's what having a home match is all about. If you are passionate about the Stars and Stripes, get to a match and cheer them on! The now infamous snow game against Costa Rica in Denver was a perfect example of using our home advantage. We could schedule a match in Barrow, Alaska next time. They have a proper pitch! Certainly, our regional competition schedules games at altitude and on less than ideal pitches during the hottest part of the day.

England's national football stadium is in northwest London. Wembley's arch rises out of the surrounding suburbs, towering over the chimneystacks and roundabouts. It must be an intimidating place to play. Not so for Poland, though. I've been told that the second-most spoken language in England is Polish.

In the final WCQ for their group in 2013, it was Poland versus England. Poland had already been eliminated from qualifying for the World Cup, and England needed victory to be assured of automatic qualification for Brazil as the Ukraine was right on their heels.

Like Mexican fans in the United States, Polish fans flocked to Wembley and supported their team with heart and bravado, creating a hybrid crowd of home and away, a celebration of the game. Sometimes the Polish supporters were louder than the English fans. In the end though, England and Liverpool's captain Steven Gerrard's eighty-eighth-minute goal gave England a 2–0 lead that silenced the Poles and gave all three points to England. It was a crucial win. The Three Lions finished just one point ahead of Ukraine in Group H of the European WCQ earning a trip to Brazil.

CHAPTER EIGHT

The Domestic and International Game

THIS SECTION LOOKS at how America's soccer does and does not fit into the broader, global game. We need to further the understanding of the game to cultivate the various levels of competition that currently exist in America. Soccer is more than the MLS or NCAA championships.

The Clubs

The many levels and competitions of football are rich, storied, and fantastic. Most Americans have a general understanding of the passion for football around the world yet still underestimate it. If you combine the passion for the NBA, NFL, MLB, and collegiate sports, you have the equivalent of soccer in Europe. It is that big. In England, rugby and cricket are distant companions. This passion is applied to the national teams as well as the FCs.

Americans don't have a solid understanding of the nuances of the sport and the various levels of competition because our major domestic sports generally only have one competition. The Dallas Cowboys and Pittsburgh Steelers want to win the Super Bowl. During a long, grueling season, a top FC may be involved in two or three competitions, perhaps more. This is true in every footballing region of the world. The longest annual competition for a FC is the normal league competition. In Europe, the top leagues by country are the English Premier League, France's League 1, Spain's La Liga, Italy's Serie A (you have to say "serie ah"), and Germany's Bundesleaga, among many others.

In North America, the top two leagues are LIGA MX in Mexico and the MLS. It should be noted that the MLS has teams from the United States and Canada. In this two-country league, Canada has three entries, Toronto FC, Vancouver Whitecaps, and Montreal Impact, the newest member to the MLS. Unlike most other soccer leagues, the MLS divides the teams into two conferences, eastern and western, due to the geographical expanse of North America.

Casual American sports fans identify with a league as it is consistent with professional baseball, American football, and basketball league formats. The league matches are played normally, but not always, on the weekend, and they play their rivals across the river or city as well as the rest of the teams in the league. American sports fans are aware of the MLS and the LA Galaxy but don't yet have an understanding of the CONCACAF Champions League.

English FCs also play for the FA Cup, a trophy won by the best English club played as a long tournament going on at the same time as the others mentioned above. The FA or Football Association is England's soccer organization.

The top prize in England is the Premier League Championship. It is awarded to the team with the most points at the end of the season. Sometimes the title is decided with weeks to go with no big final showdown between teams. Other times, the final weekend can be very dramatic. Going into the last matches of the 2011–2012 EPL season, things were still unsettled between Manchester United and Manchester City at the top of the standings, setting up a finish for the ages. Manchester City was home, playing bottom-dwelling

Queen's Park Rangers (QPR) and were two points on top. All Manchester City needed was a win to take home the title, its first in forty-four years. Manchester United were playing and beating Sunderland. Meanwhile, Manchester City found themselves losing to QPR late into the game. As time ticked toward ninety minutes, United finished off Sunderland. Stoppage time for Manchester City would require two goals to win the game, the league, and Manchester bragging rights.

In a near miraculous finish for Manchester City, they scored twice in stoppage time, two grand slams in the bottom of the ninth to win the game, a late touchdown, onside kick recovery, and an even later touchdown on a Hail Mary. This type of finish to a season, taking place simultaneously in separate stadiums, doesn't happen in America.

The best club teams in the world are currently European-based. Inevitably, these top European teams are global brands: Barcelona, Manchester United, Inter, Bayern Munich, and Real Madrid. They are recognized in America, Africa, and Asia. Even though there is a "club World Cup," which crowns the "best global club," the European powers would much rather win UEFA Champions League, the most coveted club cup in the world.

This was evident when Chelsea lost the title match of the Club World Cup to SC Corinthians Paulista of Brazil. While Chelsea wanted to win, it wasn't a top priority. Our household despises Chelsea, and we were cheering against them in the Club World Cup final because winning it didn't mean nearly as much to them as it would to the Corinthians. Good won out, and the Brazilian side celebrated while Chelsea walked off runners-up. Interestingly, this game received little coverage in Europe and almost none in the United States, even though it is the top trophy for most clubs in the world.

European teams like Real Madrid and Manchester City also play in the UEFA Champions League, a competition for the top club teams across Europe that runs almost as long as the league season but has fewer games with many breaks. The format is similar to that of the World Cup. Teams are placed into groups with the top two advancing to the next round. Once qualified out of the group, a draw takes place to determine the next matchups, which pit two teams against each other playing home and away with winner advancing. Once the competition is whittled down to two teams, like the Super Bowl, they play a one game championship match in a predetermined location.

Each country/league has different ways to qualify for Champions League, but a club generally needs to win its home country league or finish in the top two or three or win a league cup or similar type of competition.

CONCACAF's Champions League started in 2008 but was previously known as the Champions Cup, which was first contested in 1962. The current format is very similar to UEFA Champions League. Historically, teams based in the United States have done poorly, usually losing to Mexican or Costa Rican teams in the group and knockout rounds. In the early years of the competition, the entrant teams from the United States reads like a hodgepodge of proud immigrants: New York Greek America, Philadelphia Ukrainians, and New York Hungarians.

It wasn't until 1997 that a team from the United States made it to the championship match. The LA Galaxy may have lost to Cruz Azul that year, but the tides were turning. The very next year, DC United won the competition, and the Galaxy won it two years later. These were real breakthroughs for the sport in America. We need to demonstrate that we can win the regional club competitions on a consistent basis if we are to be taken seriously in the world. Real

Salt Lake lost the final in 2011 to Monterrey, a team that established itself at the top, winning again in 2012 and 2013.

The most recent edition of the competition had three MLS teams in the quarterfinals. Unlike the knockout round pairings in Europe (which are determined by chance), seeding from the groups stages determine the CONCACAF quarterfinals matchups. The team with the most points to qualify is paired off with the eighth-best team to qualify.

(6) LA Galaxy versus (3) Club Tijuana

(7) Sporting KC versus (2) Cruz Azul

(8) San Jose Earthquakes versus (1) Deportivo Toluca FC

The other contest featured Costa Rican club (5) Alajuelense versus Panamanian side (4) Club Deportivo Arabe Unido.

Unfortunately, none of the MLS teams survived this round. Cruz Azul went on to hoist the trophy in 2014 and have now won the competition more than any other team from CONCACAF.

Traveling around Europe can be much easier and is certainly more commonplace than traveling around North and Central America to watch teams compete. Kansas City to Panama anyone? Seattle to San Jose (the one in Costa Rica)? London to Paris: easy.

Many other regional, national, continental, and world competitions abound.

A Small Sampling of Other Cups

- The Cascadia Cup is played between the Vancouver Whitecaps, Portland Timbers, and Seattle Sounders in the Pacific Northwest.

- The MLS Cup is the top trophy in the MLS won by the LA Galaxy in 2012.
- The CONCACAF Gold Cup is the regional championship for the Confederation of North, Central and Caribbean Association Football.

Promotion and Relegation

The nuances of one goal between relegation and glory are lost on a nation that moves troubled teams from one city to another or keeps teams in leagues for decades when they aren't competitive in the modern era. At the same time, we love the Cinderella story potential of the NCAA brackets. (And the Pittsburgh Pirates played well in 2014!)

I love watching some of the final matches of a season between two teams at the bottom of the Premier League. It's not just about the loss of revenue. They are playing for respect and the potential that being in a top European league offers. They don't want to get relegated or "go down." It is the exact opposite of a meaningless NBA regular season game late in the season between two teams eliminated from playoff contention, aside from those playing for lottery picks. (But that just highlights how awful that procedure can be.) The tackles are a little harder, runs are a little sharper, and fans are a whole lot more boisterous.

Alas, the owners of American professional sports teams would never allow this type of promotion and relegation system to be implemented now. We could press on Congress and the president to get it started. Remember the playoff system Obama was talking about in college football? Let's use Twitter and Facebook to get going! This is far more important to sports culture in America than a disputed NCAA national football championship.

The most obvious candidates for a promotion and relegation system would be baseball and hockey. They already have lower, non-collegiate levels of competition so only minor tinkering of the systems would need to happen. The "feeder" system in baseball would need to change.

Cue dream sequence. Relegation is initiated for the 2017 MLB season!

Sadly, the Yankees are having an off year. A-Ro(i)d is thankfully just about done with his career, and he and assorted Yankee company are at Fenway for the final series of the season. The Yankees need to sweep the Red Sox to stave off relegation. The Red Sox didn't make the playoffs, and they are sitting in the middle of the AL East at 79–80. Now we have a meaningful late season series between two baseball powers. The Yankees won game one 5–1, scoring all five runs in the first two innings to set the tone. Game two was a pitching duel seeing the Yankees win 2–0, setting up an epic battle in the final game of the season. Could you imagine the atmosphere? It's more intense than a playoff game. One last game. One last chance to vanquish the Yankees out of the top flight of MLB for at least a season! The AAA Iron Pigs already won promotion. It's either the Yankees or Mariners on the way down. How great would that feel for Red Sox Nation? Would they miss the Yankees next season? I don't think so, knowing the Yankees would most likely win promotion the following season. They would spend money like drunken sailors to get back to the show. So the rivalry would just take a holiday and then be renewed with vigor. And a really pissed-off Yankee team would be back. I can dream, right?

The MLS needs to put a promotion and relegation system in place before more time passes and establish a lower league. An agreement needs to be established between the MLS and the current NASL. It is highly unlikely at this time, but both leagues would benefit greatly from it. Clearly, the MLS is the dominant soccer league in the United States, and NASL isn't going to compete at the same level. Instead of letting the MLS poach the top teams from the NASL, they could just be friends. The Montreal Impact used to play in the NASL but gained "promotion" through negotiation.

Playoffs, Knockouts, and Other Fun Formats to Award a Champion

Playoffs are in just about every professional sports league in America, including soccer, yet are absent in the global game in how they follow a regular season. In America, teams compete in a regular season to qualify for the playoffs and then advance through the playoffs to a championship game or series: World Series, NBA Finals, Stanley Cup, and Super Bowl. (The most notable and famous exclusion would be the NCAA American football championship, where a computer decides the teams playing in the final.) Regular season yields playoffs, which yields a championship. That is the normal, linear flow of an American sports seasons. Again, if you don't qualify for the playoffs, there isn't much to cheer about aside from maybe playing spoiler or getting a decent pick in the next draft.

The format for determining a champion is different for soccer. UEFA and CONCACAF Champions Leagues play out in a format similar to the group stage/knockout stage format the World Cup employs. In this type of format, every team plays a minimum number of group games against all the other teams in the same group with a certain number of teams advancing out of the group to a knockout stage. In the World Cup, the knockout stage is single elimination with everyone, save the host country, playing an essentially neutral game.

In other competitions, the knockout stages are a two-game head-to-head series with each team hosting a game. Away goals scored are weighted more than home goals. If the two games end up with scores of 2–1 and 1–0 with the games won and goals scored even, the team that scored more away goals wins.

If you asked an American soccer player if he would rather win the MLS Cup or World Cup, it wouldn't even be close. Or if you asked a European player if he'd rather win Champions League or World Cup, it would be the same (unless you are a tiny handful of Spanish players who have won the World Cup and haven't been on a Champions League-winning club team).

PART 3

Where We Could Be

CHAPTER NINE

Create More Passionate Fans

MERICA NEEDS MORE soccer fans. Without passionate fans, the quest for America to win the World Cup is futile. Fans support the teams, players, and sport, which will in turn improve the level of competition and ultimately the quality of the players on the pitch. This is the single most important factor to contribute to America's quest to win the World Cup. This will in turn lead to a stronger domestic league, the second important criteria to creating a world-class team.

Woven through the chapters of this book are anecdotes from a gradually shifting sports and cultural landscape in America. People are beginning to see the game as our own and embracing it like never before.

America clearly supports sport. We have passionate baseball, basketball, and American football fans. One can argue that collegiate sports generate some of the most passionate fans, especially in football and basketball towns. In England, every town has a FC, and at a minimum, folks follow the team loosely. In America, collegiate athletics, notably American football and basketball, serve this area in sports society. People in Boise, Idaho, know how the Boise State University football team is doing even if they don't go to the games or are rabid football fans. It's the same for Auburn, Alabama, as well as many other college towns in America. Boise and

Auburn have no professional sports team, so the college teams have minimal competition.

In Chapel Hill, North Carolina, home of the University of North Carolina Tar Heels, the town goes nuts when the Duke Blue Devils basketball team pays a visit. ESPN rides into town to televise an in-state collegiate basketball game to the nation and around the world.

Imagine if, instead of football in Boise and Auburn or basketball in Indiana and North Carolina, the soccer teams generated such a following: packed stadiums, local pride, rivalries, and buildup to the games, all for soccer. It is starting to happen in MLS cities for the professional clubs and in selected areas around the country, but it's not widespread yet. The all-encompassing nature of the game in these towns can be grown, nurtured, and developed with soccer fans in other towns. Cities such as Houston, Seattle, Los Angeles, St. Louis, Philadelphia, and Bradenton, Florida, are known as soccer hotbeds with robust competition and quality coaching.

Slowly, soccer highlights from the MLS and other leagues around the world are creeping into the daily top-ten plays on the evening cable news shows. This is part of the cultural shift. Soccer has been played in the United States and around for world for generations, but it is just now starting to crack the regular broadcast lineup. Even the sports score ticker on ESPN will feature top European teams and mention when an American (or Mexican like Javier Hernandez for Real Madrid) player does something noteworthy. With cable and internet delivery, people are also able to watch teams from all regions of the world. Creating more fans will help the MLS continue to build its brand.

The MLS has done a great job of creating a distinct soccer culture for fans, and now the games are being televised on a regular basis. What really helps is having people connect with players. The game in America only gets elevated when players like Thierry Henry, Jermaine DeFoe, and Michael Bradley decide to come to the MLS. And it's great when American MLS players make the jump to the national team.

A little unintentional cross marketing doesn't hurt, like what happened in 2013 during the Gold Cup. Eddie Johnson, a striker for the Seattle Sounders, started playing for Team USA during the USMNT romp. The USMNT played a game in Seattle, and Eddie Johnson scored a goal for the national team while playing on his club team's turf. What a brilliant way to solidify his popularity and cross-market the MLS and USMNT at the same time.

This is a unique opportunity in American sports. Our national basketball teams don't play meaningful games on domestic soil on a regular basis. We certainly get behind them for the Olympics, but that is about it. And the NFL has no national team. Could you imagine a World Cup for American football? Me neither.

On the national level, there is room along with the NFL, NBA, NHL, and MLB for soccer. But can the MLS generate a large and sustainable fan base to produce quality soccer on the pitch week in and week out? Can national youth leagues and the MLS produce a steady crop of world-class soccer players? The answers to the above questions: Yes.

(Chipotle Mexican Grill just signed on as sponsor of the Homegrown Game. It's mission is to cultivate youth soccer in America and showcase some of the homegrown talent we are starting to produce in a game played during the MLS All-Star Break. This is brilliant and exactly what we need!)

The trick is linking interest in soccer at the youth level with the collegiate, club, and national level to create more players and fans so, even if players drop out of playing, they can stay interested in the sport as fans. Keep the soccer families involved.

We have a great start, and we have an entire demographic ready to help. I'm not sure how I could write a book about soccer and America and not reference a modern, urban creature. Soccer mom (or soccer parent) exists in America, and unlike Bigfoot or the chupacabra, you can see the soccer mom in parks on Saturdays or the six and seven o'clock weeknight games and training sessions. The soccer mom is a strong demographic, voting bloc, influential consumer, and agent of change for good in America. They've been used to sell minivans by the shipload!

Usually, the minivan commercial contains images of four or five kids climbing out of the vehicle to run onto a perfectly manicured green field of soccer dreams. Then the soccer mom pulls out a mesh bag of soccer balls that easily fit into the well-appointed, roomy vehicle. The minivan even has room for a cooler (or a built-in cooler if you go for the LX version) to provide the healthy drinks and peanut- or gluten-free snacks for the kids to kick butt on the pitch. The soccer mom cheers her players from the sidelines, trying to motivate her offspring to challenge for the ball before happily driving off in her super-cool wheels.

Soccer parents are also buying into the sport. Slowly, the parents gain an understanding of the game beyond favorite U-7 tactics including "kick the ball as hard as you can in any direction," "cluster ball," "weeding the turf," and "bumblebee soccer."

No longer is soccer in America seen as an alternative for kids if they don't make the basketball or football team. This is important because some of these kids are choosing soccer as their number-one sport, not a fallback that will just get them some exercise. Additionally, as exposure of the sport increases, whether it's going to an MLS match or watching the English Premier League on TV, they will began to shift their ambition. When I was growing up, everybody wanted to be like Mike (Michael Jordon). Now I see kids emulating Messi and Ronaldo. (Hopefully one day, they will want to be like an American soccer player.)

Playing and learning the game at a grassroots level also allows people to enjoy the sport recreationally as they age. They become involved, coach, and start the follow the sport. We need these types of fans.

CHAPTER TEN

Create World-Class Football Players

I F CREATING PASSIONATE fans is paramount to building a sustained high level of soccer culture in the United States, a close second is creating a fantastic product on the pitch. Consistently creating high-level players has been a problem for the USMNT. Currently, Europe sees the MLS as a place for European players past their prime to ride off into the sunset, to make a few more dollars, and to extend their career.

Granted, the MLS is certainly on the ascendancy and should continue to lure players who aren't so far past their prime from Europe and South America. In ten or fifteen years, the MLS could start to rival the big leagues around the world. Why is this important? We need a strengthening domestic league to cultivate better players. It's also important so our own US players don't have to seek European pastures to fine-tune their skill.

Surprisingly, the United States didn't have a coordinated, focused soccer development academy until 2007. It was created to provide a competitive environment for the country's elite youth soccer players. It is now starting to produce dividends as we see players that have come through the system playing professionally.

This is a great next step. In 2013, the academy is reaching thirteen- and fourteen-year-olds.

We are also starting to produce football talent that can compete with the rest of the world on an individual basis. Joshua Pynadath, an eleven-year-old from Los Altos Hills, California, became the first American to join Real Madrid's youth program. This is another incremental step forward for American soccer. Having Joshua play in Spain not only develops his talent but helps showcase American soccer to a football mad part of the world.

Joshua told the *Los Altos Town Crier,*

> Both trials were very serious, as kids are fighting to either keep a spot or to earn a spot. It was a very good feeling to be able to play well against this top competition since the level and speed of play over there is amazing. I was blown away when I got the official news from Real Madrid. They told me that I was the first American that they have ever accepted into their academy. I told them that I would set a good example.

On his time spent with Madrid's rivals (FC Barcelona), the Cristiano Ronaldo fan added, "I enjoyed my time at Barcelona. I was happy to hear the coaches tell me that I was a very good player and that I improved every day of the trial."[15]

Hey, world, we can play football and football, and here is one of our top talents playing alongside yours. It tells the scouts to keep looking to the sunny skies of California, the great plains of the

---

[15]   http://www.dailymail.co.uk/sport/football/article-2383081/Real-Madrid-beat-Barcelona-signing-11-year-old-American-Joshua-Pynadath.html

Midwest, and the big cities for talent. Joshua's move also shows that scouts are looking to the United States more and more, even if his coach in California sent tapes of him playing to Spain! He also had a tryout with Barcelona's youth academy. Clearly, he is a very talented kid. His family was willing to move to Madrid to support him and invest in his ability. Now, more space in our sports society is being created to nurture players domestically.

In early September 2013, the *Philadelphia Union* announced the opening of a development high school for kids to focus on academics and football training, giving the kids a connectedness and pathway to the higher levels of the sport. These academies in America also move the community focus more toward soccer.

Imagine youths peering through a fence at night to watch the kids in the academy playing. The kids get inspired, interested, and connected to the global game and get invited on the other side of the fence to watch and try out. Instead of playing basketball or football, the next time they get together with friends, they might have a kick-a-bout. It could be any city.

Soccer balls replace footballs and baseballs at the family picnic. The kids take an interest in the local team and get tickets to a match. Soccer may not become the number one sport for a while, but it can nudge itself into the top four.

The continued growth of the MLS is crucial as it provides an avenue for homegrown players to have clear visibility to an end goal: having a domestic professional career. Even just having athletes to look up to, to poster the walls with, is crucial. Kids will need to choose to play soccer over other sports.

Train More Coaches in America

In order to train better players, America needs more top-level coaches who understand the game. We need to continue to build coaching at the grassroots level with a broad base to support an ever-higher reaching pinnacle of US coaching.

Our diversity will help improve coaching at all levels. Different regions and countries have differing styles of play. We can further incorporate varying coaching styles and tactics and make it our own. Neither do we have a legacy of a style with deep history and traditions to shake off or try to adjust.

I coached for a couple years in Anchorage and then was drawn back into it in England. I received my FA level 1 coaching certifications. From that point on, I was hooked. My older son and I talk tactics about the U-10 teams and the Premier League. What's the difference for a coach?

We love watching the different styles of players with defensive-minded midfielders, attacking wingback/defenders to bulldozing or finesse strikers. Once you understand the game at a slightly deeper level, you really see the mental side of the game come out in the differing styles.

These experiences aggregated shifted my love of sport from baseball and American football to soccer. Am I just becoming a victim of cultural assimilation? I don't think so. The game of soccer has always captivated me. I just needed the right outlet.

Tactics and Lineups for USMNT

Four-four-two, four-five-one, and four-three-three, all are some of the popular modern lineups employed by most club and country teams. It's four on the backline, about the same in the midfield, and usually a smaller number attacking.

Tactics in the future for the USMNT will depend on the types of players we produce. As the game continues to evolve higher, there isn't a reason why we can't produce a Ronaldo-type of player, lightning quick, smart, and technically world class. Granted, the "technically world class" will take time and nurturing at the grassroots level. But it is attainable, and again, will ultimately happen by harnessing the strength of America, our diversity. Take from the melting pot the best, train them to the highest level, give them confidence and a willingness to take risk, then wrap them in our workmanlike ethos and can-do American spirit. This is how we build.

Historically, we have relied on a solid keeper and a strong work ethic. Think Casey Keller with solid defense and satisfactory midfield. We've never had a world-class striker capable of captivating the opposition. The philosophy against stronger opponents has looked like "Don't let the other team score, hold possession, and counter quickly," as in the 2009 Confederations Cup final. The United States can get out of the CONCACAF easily and has. But we need to elevate the game at the World Cup. The rest of it is meaningless. We need a hard back line and very smart midfield.

The great European and South American teams all have distinct styles of play, and we need to emulate certain aspects of each. America does have a style of play, and we need to continue to find the right players to not only fit into the system but also to push the system in new directions for an American team. We are known for strong, hardworking players that may not be the most technically skilled. That is where we can improve our game the most.

Belief

Jurgen Klinnsman has the team playing extremely well, the players are buying into his system, and they are starting to believe. They have to believe they can compete at the top level in order to win at the top level. In 2013 and 2014, they played very difficult friendly matches against World Cup-bound European teams: Germany, Belgium, Italy, France, and Bosnia-Herzegovina with some success.

Unfortunately, they are only friendlies. We only face the big boys in meaningful matches in the World Cup or Confederations Cup when there is no room for error.

We have to believe that we can compete with the top teams. Both the fans and the players know it. Part of what Jurgen Klinnsman brings is his street credit. That credit, combined with his belief in the players, can elevate our game even more.

We Have the Demographics

If numbers can back up belief, it can be even more powerful. The United States has demographics and diversity in our favor. Consider the following table in terms of population and success in the global game:

Country	Population	World Cups	Runners-up	3rd place
Uruguay	3 million	2	0	0
Netherlands	17 million	0	3	0
Spain	47 million	1	0	0
Italy	61 million	4	2	1
France	65 million	1	1	2
Brazil	197 million	5	2	2
USA	314 million	0	0	1

Uruguay hosted and won the inaugural World Cup in 1930, and they also won in 1950 and looked really good in 2010. And the Netherlands! I know. I'm sorry. Dutch fans! You battled Spain all the way to the final in 2010. Spain is surprising with only one title. But they also won back-to-back European championships in 2008 and 2012, sandwiching that World Cup win, an incredible run. That gets lost in North America. The current Spanish side is arguably the greatest national football team to take the pitch. Their dominance was certainly tested in Brazil and they will have to reinvent themselves. Even before the World Cup in Brazil they begun to show signs of vulnerability, most notably getting beat 4–0 by Brazil in the Confederation Cup Final in 2013. And yes, the United States beat Spain in the Confederations Cup as well in 2009, the World Cup warm-up tournament for each regional winner in 2009 right after they won Euro 2008 and before they raised the 2010 World Cup trophy.

Uruguay is currently ranked seventh in the world, according to the Coca-Cola FIFA world rankings, and it has a population under 4 million. (The greater LA Metro area has almost 18 million people.) Uruguay continues to produce world-class footballers at a fantastic per capita rate.

Another national team that sparks interest in my family is Iceland. They made it out of the group qualification of Europe and lost to Croatia in the playoffs for a World Cup spot. Iceland's population is 320,000 people, roughly the same size as my hometown of Anchorage, Alaska. Could the city of Anchorage put together a team that would compete with Croatia for a spot in Brazil? Not likely, but the point is, with a huge population, America should do better. We have the demographics.

America also has certain policy advantages that would help football ascend to higher levels. It's a touchy political topic, but immigration does help the economy, and it also helps soccer. "Give us your tired, your poor, your huddled masses yearning to be free." And if they come with a culture of football, even better!

America is a melting pot, tapestry, or whatever you what to call it: Haitian Americans, German Americans, Ghanian Americans, Kenyan Americans, Icelandic Americans, Mexican Americans. We are all Americans. If you put on the Stars and Stripes, let it rip. Jurgen Klinnsmann talks about the different styles of play that people bring to the country and the US national teams. In the long run, this will be a strength for the team.

The single most important factor in creating a program that competes and sustains itself in among the top-ten national teams in the world starts with getting some of our best athletes into soccer instead of American football or basketball. We need a Michael Jordon or Wayne Gretzky of soccer.

CHAPTER ELEVEN

Host the World Cup Tournament Again

HOSTING PROVIDES AN amazing boost to the home team. England and France have won the World Cup once each, only winning the one time they hosted. Argentina has won the World Cup twice, once as hosts.

Further to the point, only teams that have hosted a World Cup have actually won, although not always at the same time. And only eight countries have ever won the World Cup: Brazil, Italy, (West) Germany, Argentina, Uruguay, England, France, and Spain.

Year	Host	Winner
1930	Uruguay	Uruguay
1934	Italy	Italy
1938	France	Italy (second win)
1950	Brazil	Uruguay (second win)
1954	Switzerland	West Germany
1958	Sweden	Brazil
1962	Chile	Brazil (second win)
1966	England	England
1970	Mexico	Brazil (third win)

1974	West Germany	West Germany (second win)
1978	Argentina	Argentina
1982	Spain	Italy (third win)
1986	Mexico	Argentina (second win)
1990	Italy	West Germany (third win)
1994	United States	Brazil (fourth win)
1998	France	France
2002	Japan and South Korea	Brazil (fifth win)
2006	Germany	Italy (fourth win)
2010	South Africa	Spain
2014	Brazil	Germany (fourth win)
2018	Russia	
2022	Qatar[16]	

South Africa was the first host nation not to progress from the group stages.

Selecting the World Cup Host Nation(s)

The problem this faces for America is that the selection process for choosing the host nation(s), like the Olympic selection, is a total racket and plays right into international bias against American soccer. Corruption and bribery scandals also taint it. The selection for 2018 and 2022 happened at the same time, so it's easy to see how this system could encourage a you-vote-for-me-in-2018-and-I-vote-for-you-in-2022 alliance. During the official selection process that determined the 2018 and 2022 hosts, two members of FIFA's executive committee had voting rights suspended after allegations of a money-for-votes scheme. Shocking!

---

[16]   Current selection to host

Russia won the selection process, and it is hosting the 2018 World Cup. Russia will do fine. (Check that. Some Russians will do fine.) The oligarchs who made billions from the Sochi Olympics stand to do the same for the World Cup. The Olympics were just a warm-up for the World Cup for Russia. Okay, Russia gets the World Cup in 2018.

All cheekiness aside, on the pitch, the current Russian teams and former Soviet Union teams over the last sixty years are very competitive. The Soviet team consistently made it to the quarterfinals of the World Cups, finishing as high as fourth in 1966. The current Russian team qualified for the 2014 World Cup as winners of European Group F, topping Portugal by one point. (Portugal then had to beat Sweden in a playoff to qualify for Brazil in a match that featured two of the best players in the world, Christiano Ronaldo and Zlatan Ibrohimovich.) However, for the World Cup in Brazil, Russia wasn't drawn into a Group of Death but failed to produce as Belgium and Algeria advanced leaving Russia (and South Korea, the other team not to advance) out of the knock-out rounds.

Surely the United States will get to host the 2022 tournament? Among other contenders to host in either 2018 or 2022, the United States lost 2022 as well. With help from legendary Frenchman Zidane and other political influences, Qatar won. Qatar, a country with just over 250,000 citizens, minimal infrastructure, a ruling class, and one of the clearest examples of a modern caste system, is hosting. The other 1.75 million listed in the official state of Qatar population are foreign workers toiling for the ruling class.

Qatar is planning to build nine new stadiums for the World Cup, each with a forty thousand-plus capacity. All Qatari citizens could easily fit into the seats of the new stadiums at the same time with room to spare. Of all the countries that have hosted and never won a World Cup (Switzerland, Sweden, Chile, Mexico, United

States, South Korea, Japan, and South Africa), Qatar will seem the least likely to hoist the trophy. And hosting the tournament will be the best chance for them to win the tournament as they haven't ever qualified for a World Cup Final before.

Qatar is hot in the summer with normal July temperatures reaching 40-plus Celsius (104-plus Fahrenheit). Concern over the safety of the players may see the tournament moved to the winter months. Sadly, the safety of the workers building the stadiums and infrastructure is less of a concern as they toil in peak temperatures. This goes far beyond a befuddled American soccer fan. It comes down to human rights.

> The European Parliament is the latest body to denounce Qatar's treatment of migrant workers with a powerful demand to the authorities to radically improve human rights and put an end to "forced and slave labour."

> United Nations officials, Amnesty International and string of other human rights organizations and trade unions have all exposed the scale of the problem in recent days as the pressure mounts on the 2022 World Cup host nation to act swiftly to reform working conditions and living standards and stop the withdrawal of wages.[17]

FIFA should be held accountable for awarding the World Cup to a nation with abysmal labor laws bordering (kafala system) on "slave labor." Reports are surfacing, detailing over one thousand

---

17 www.insideworldfootball.com/world-cup/62-qatar/

construction workplace deaths since the announcement of the Qatar winning bid. Certainly, FIFA wants to showcase the biggest tournament to all parts of the globe. So I'm sure China will appropriately host the men's tournament in the next twenty to thirty years.

On FIFA's website are virtuous mission statements. Their approach is to "build a better future":

> Football is no longer considered merely a global sport, but also as unifying force whose virtues can make an important contribution to society. We use the power of football as a tool for social and human development, by strengthening the work of dozens of initiatives around the globe to support local communities in the areas of peace building, health, social integration, education and more.[18]

Sepp Blatter, please adhere to your mission and use the power of football to support the workers who are building these beautiful stadiums.

---

[18] http://www.fifa.com/aboutfifa/organisation/mission.html

PART FOUR

Shifting the Culture
(and other stuff)

CHAPTER TWELVE

Changing Allegiance

THIS IS ONE story of how an American, an Alaskan, grew up a baseball and football fan and converted. Baseball still holds a special place, as all first loves do, but the global passion of soccer overwhelmed it. It was an avalanche that came down and quenched a global thirst that mainstream American sports can't.

I was born in 1974 in Anchorage, Alaska. We have no top-level professional sports teams and are about a thousand miles from nowhere. America does have several hotbeds for soccer, and Alaska is not one of them. We have northern lights, lots of snow and ice, polar and grizzly bears, whales, hunting, fishing, and all the other Alaskan-y stuff people normally associate with the state. Growing up, I enjoyed the sports that were available to me: hiking, fishing, dip netting (not really a sport as it involves sticking a net into the river and scooping out salmon), both types of skiing, and, yes, soccer. Downhill skiing was a passion, and we learned to ski on a very hard, steep mountain that was more often than not fraught with icy conditions. Before the parabolic skis came around, we had 208- and 210-centimeter racing boards that were very rigid and sharp, built for cruising and carving the ice.

As a kid, I played for a local recreational soccer team, and I was invited to try out for the competitive team. Tryouts for the "comp" team were paralyzing. Giants were calmly juggling the ball, blasting shots at helpless goalies rotating in, and knocking down scrawny "tryout" kids like me. Somehow I made it on the competitive team and then faded into junior high obscurity. I have few memories of scoring goals for the junior high team, but they were scrappy garbage goals, cleaning up in front of the net. More importantly, I remember taking road trips with the team. We once drove the four hundred miles to Fairbanks from Anchorage in an RV for a statewide soccer tournament. Eating junk food and hanging out with fellow teammates along the way was priceless.

Playing soccer in America in the 1980s, you could sense the global aspect of the game. We were playing a sport that was a tier below the big American sports but was by far the most popular game in the world. Even everyone in remote Alaska knew Pelé and Maradona, and we also knew that Brazil and Italy usually won the World Cup.

I also played intramural football at university, and I still play five-a-side football a couple nights a week. Think indoor rules soccer played in a squared ice hockey rink (without the ice of course) with a large semicircle ice hockey-style crease that neither the goalie can leave nor any player can enter. It's a smashing game, and sometimes I'm not the worst player on the pitch, but usually I am. I play the game for fun. I loved it and still do. The older dudes who play are amazing with little flicks and touches. I can't get the ball off them for the life of me and usually just run around in circles.

It's far better than a treadmill. Sometimes they make an errant pass, and I latch on to the ball. It makes it all worthwhile. But they are still playing, some fifty or sixty years old. Surely some of the younger lads group me in with the "older dudes" category, but they can get the ball off me.

During warm ups and after the game, they banter about their teams.

"It looks like it is Liverpool's year."

"Did you see that goal Toure [Yaya Toure, an Ivorian International player] scored? Unbelievable."

"Suarez is on fire! Let's hope he doesn't get too hungry."

Like talking about the weather in England, bringing up football is a nice way of making small talk, and these guys are pros.

Baseball and Softball

Because soccer received little to no coverage in Alaska, baseball first got me intrigued as a sports fan. Actually, the numbers baited the hook. Watching batting averages, RBIs, stolen bases, standings, and ERA change on a daily basis was fascinating. Somehow over time, what an ERA means clarified to me completely. This was before the days of WHIP, which is a fairly easy one to figure out (walks and hits per innings pitched). AL and NL box scores packed the sports pages of the *Anchorage Daily News*. This was long before the days of instantaneous highlights, 24-7 access to all things sports on cable, and the Internet accessed now from virtually any device anywhere.

I had to go to the front door, pull the orange plastic bag off the newspaper, and spread it on the kitchen table. My breakfast was usually a bowl of cereal and a complete pouring over of the box scores from the previous day's games. When I was feeling nasty like Miss Jackson, I jammed four Eggo waffles into the toaster and ate them with an intricate layering of butter and Aunt Jemima syrup. (Sorry, Mrs. Butterworth, but your bottle shape kind of weirded me out. I felt like you just wanted me to be chubby and lovable like you or John Kruk.) After a win for the Phils, I was on cloud nine.

After a morning cup of coffee in the form of a little W, all was right in the world!

From Anchorage, the nearest professional sports teams were in Vancouver and Seattle (thirteen hundred and fourteen hundred air miles, respectively). The Seahawks, Mariners, and Sonics were big in Anchorage, but the natural contrarian in me had me seeking other outlets. Maybe I should have checked out the Vladivostok team, FC Luch-Energiya. They weren't so far away geographically, and they play in the Siberia Premier League, but that was when things weren't so warm and fuzzy between my country and the Union of Soviet Socialist Republics. We would get reports in the local newspaper of the Russians flying planes into Alaskan airspace, testing how long it took our F-15s to scramble and intercept. The neighborhood kids I grew up with were hoping for a *Top Gun* incident right over the skies of Anchorage with Maverick defending America and the last frontier from the Russians right over our heads! A missile from the F-15 hits the MiG right before the Russian pilot ejects. What was left of the plane slams into Flat Top Mountain in the Chugach range. Or not. Nothing that exciting ever happens in Anchorage.

There was nothing in the newspaper about soccer except the occasional high school score line in August or September. I'd open the paper and go to section C or D and spend most of the bright Alaskan summer mornings pouring over the numbers.

Little League baseball was in Anchorage, but none of my friends played. Somebody gave me a black Don Mattingly glove that was rarely used to catch a ball but initially found employment as a doorstop or paperweight. It did get some use when I was a teenager and young adult playing slow-pitch softball, an all-American pastime full of people with big dreams playing them out in beer leagues. I started my softball career playing for my dad's team of plus-forty guys called the Limp Sticks. (I am not making this up.) I was fourteen years old playing beer league softball. We played in the lowest men's league in the city, and the only home runs hit were because it was a single with a three-base error. Significant and extremely important rules were added to the game, including:

1. The person who made the final out of the game had to bring a case of beer to the next game.
2. If you struck out (remember, it's slow-pitch), you had to bring a case of beer to the next game.

One season, we played in a league with a prison team. The prison team didn't have away games. In order to make the trip behind bars, we had to go through background checks, which meant that not everyone on our team made the trip to the other side. Outstanding parking tickets and back city taxes were enough to deter some to play. Hopefully, nobody was dodging more heinous crimes. Anyway, the prison players were cordial and quite good, and I'm pretty sure they won the league that year. I guess they had lots of time to practice. Thankfully, they weren't in our league most years.

Setting the Hook as a Sports Fan

When I was a kid, I hadn't ever been to a professional sporting event. I dreamed of living near an MLB park, walking to the games, watching batting practice, soaking up the sun, and generally being a bum in the bleachers. But I can't complain. My first experience at a major sporting event was certainly grand: the 1984 LA Olympic Games. My mother worked for ABC networks as a temporary Olympic employee, and we spent the summer living at my aunt, uncle, and cousins' home in Long Beach, California. Aside from playing in the surf all day and going to Disneyland, I remember attending two Olympic events: soccer and track and field.

My dad and I got to see France versus Egypt in the knockout rounds at the Rose Bowl in Pasadena. France won that match 2–0 and eventually the gold medal over Brazil in the final. It was the first time I had that feeling of being in a mass of people cheering and sharing an experience. It is still with me.

Back in Alaska, I talked my mother into getting basic cable and could occasionally catch the Phillies on WGN when playing the Cubs or on TBS when playing the Braves. Like so many others, I also fell for the lovable Wrigley legend Harry Caray: "Ah one, ah two, ah, take me out to the ballgame…" I even cheered for the Cubs with Dunston and Sandberg when they weren't playing the Phils.

America's pastime is fun with its history, characters, and quirkiness. I could have just as easily ended up cheering for my dad's other team, the Cleveland Indians, but something deep down inside me knew I needed to cheer for the ultimate underdog, a team approaching ten thousand losses, a team (at the time) with only one World Series title in over a hundred years. Lucky me. Even with a full 162 games a year, ten thousand losses is a fantastic achievement.

A few years later, tragedy struck. The Phils made it to the World Series representing the National League against the Toronto Blue Jays of the American League. My dad and I were watching game six of the 1993 World Series from a large sofa in Anchorage with other Philly fans. Watching Mitch "Wild Thing" Williams give up the bomb to Joe Carter in that very un-baseball-like stadium was devastating. The Phils lost the World Series on a walk-off home run. Is there a more spectacular way to lose?

I remember thinking that all they needed was a ground ball and double play and it would be back to Philly for game seven of the World Series where the Phils would wrap it up. Ugh! As a fan, that loss was devastating. I was sure they would win it. All that time wasted on the Phils. I'd invested so many mornings and memorized so many stats, lineups, and pitching rotations. How could they not pay me back? It was a long offseason. The highlight of Joe Carter's walk-off home run still gets aired sometimes, and it still stings a little.

It taught me loyalty and the fact that a fan stays with the team. There's no jumping ship. Redemption took fifteen years, a decade and a half of ups and downs. Okay, it was mostly downs. I remember that feeling, watching the Phils finish off the Tampa Bay Devil Rays after some wacky rain delays for the World Series title. I called my dad. We celebrated. It was muted seeing as we were older and wiser, but we celebrated. I knew that once I picked a team or club, I wasn't going to switch.

All those years of toiling as a fan, reading morning newspapers and message board smack talking, and enduring those ten thousand losses, it was all worth it. We won. And I'm glad I'm not a Cubs fan. But when it comes to cheering for your country, you don't really have a choice.

The Seattle Mariners and Sounders: Modern Lessons Learned

In the summer of 2010, I was in Seattle with my family for a combo work/play trip. I managed to squeeze in a Mariners game and a Sounders match. It was a pivotal time for my personal sports allegiances.

A group of people I was working with at the time went to the Mariners game. I hadn't been to a baseball game for a couple years, and I was looking forward to the smell of the grass and hearing the sound of the bat and the pop of the catcher's mitt. My previous baseball outing was with my sister in Pittsburgh to see the Pirates take on my beloved Phils. All was as it should be in Pittsburgh.

Safeco Field was not even half full, and the Mariners were losing well over half their games. I'm a baseball fan, and this was a boring game. The Mariners were complete rubbish with Little League errors and swinging at garbage pitches. It was over by the fifth inning, and even a couple more ten-dollar beers couldn't eliminate the pit in my stomach. Nothing a little fundamental practice and perhaps better scouting couldn't fix, I guess. Or at least someone pitching in the three, four, and five spots of the rotation that might win a game occasionally.

But I began to notice things at this game. A sense of dread began to creep up on me as I realized something deeper and more sinister about the modern fan experience. This wasn't how it was supposed to be. I could handle the loss, but the culture of the game had changed. Going to a stadium to talk business and drink while there happened to be a game taking place? I felt myself drifting out of the conversation about software rollouts and strategic planning every time a Mariner had a three-ball count. I was the only one who was a fan of the game so I naturally tuned out the business chat as much as I could.

"Take a pitch for crying out loud! It's three and oh. Try to get into their bullpen."

"Get on base already, lousy. It's the sixth inning, and we haven't had a base runner?"

"What? Oh no no. I tested the software, and it wasn't that smooth."

"Why did you swing at that pitch?"

"Huh? Oh, right. Um, let's see. I think the data migration and subsequent testing would take maybe two to three weeks before even considering a full-scale rollout."

"Where are the peanuts and cracker jacks?"

"Are you blind, ump?"

I felt my retirement dreams of living near a stadium, walking to the home game, and maybe even keeping score slipping away with each pitch. I want the crowd to really feel it, to appreciate the history of the ballplayers of yesteryear that toiled for the love of the game. I wanted the fans to feel the agony. Don't just shrug your shoulders and down the last sip of warm beer from a plastic cup. As I looked around, I saw casual business travelers in pleated khakis, taking full advantage of the tax deduction. Where was the passion? Where were the rally caps? Where was the anger at a horrible team with bad management?

A few years before, my sister and I attended a Pirates versus Phillies game in Pittsburgh. This game had a full stadium with interested masses. We walked to the stadium along the river with thousands of other baseball fans. I realized I was part of the problem for the Mariners and the broader aspect of the game. It had turned into a soulless business outing.

Certainly not all MLB teams have to cater to the business crowd. The Chicago Cubs still play day games at iconic Wrigley Field. Even today when you tune in to watch a Cubs game on TV, you see the excitement of the fans drinking beer and soaking up the sun. They are part of the game. They are the game. At the same time, I have no illusions that the price tag of box seats complete with rolling drink (and shots) carts help the bottom line for the teams. You can get loaded after work or while traveling for business and enjoy the game while inking your next deal.

A few days after the Mariners experience, I purchased three tickets to the Seattle Sounders match from an online agent as the game was sold out. Saying it was "sold out" was a little misleading. The Sounders were playing in the Seahawks stadium, but they didn't open the upper deck. Yet, even without anyone in the upper deck, the game had an electric feel. We arrived and collected the tickets, and we were told we would be standing behind one of the goals in the "singing" section. We were given small placards with the lyrics to the songs and chants and then took our seats. Flags were waving, and people were singing and chanting, paying respects to the game and Casey Keller, the legendary American goalkeeper finishing his career as a Sounder. Casey Keller chants were a favorite of the crowd that season and picked up whenever he made a save. We only sat down at halftime. The crowd would ebb and flow with the players.

One of my favorite aspects of the game is when a team slows down the game and builds play from the back line. The Sounders orchestrated that style a few times, creating chances for their forwards. The fans feel the anticipation that this building up of play brings. The Sounders won 2–1, and the game was nonstop. We left hoarse and tired. I was spent but still giddy from the experience.

This match in Seattle planted the seed. We walked in as curious observers and left as thirsty fans. For me, it stood in stark contrast to the baseball game a few days earlier and really changed my perspective of sports in America. I may have harbored subconscious cynicism toward baseball for a few years, and this Seattle experience seemed to bring it out of me. Perhaps it was the betrayal of Mark McGwire and Barry Bonds?

Later that summer, back in Alaska, we watched as many matches of the 2010 World Cup as we could, given the time difference between South Africa and Alaska. When coaching, I used the tactics of the Dutch and Spanish to help educate my six-year-old players. I know I didn't get through to all of them, but for some, their interest was piqued. They would come to the next practice and excitedly tell me about the match they watched.

One morning, we all slept in, only to find the six-year-old had gotten himself up to watch Argentina and Germany. It had begun. I can think of no other example of a pure fan than a child waking up at 6 am on a summer morning to watch the magic of the World Cup.

CHAPTER THIRTEEN

American Football and Football

A MERICAN FOOTBALL IS still a huge sport within the borders of the United States. The NFL and NCAA have a decent partnership and pathway for players to go pro after college. It keeps people engaged with the players as they watch someone progress to the top level through the NFL draft. Soccer does have a similar mechanism, but it isn't widely distributed and consumed yet like the extravaganza that is NFL draft day.

The NFL is trying to spread the game around the world by hosting regular season games overseas. In 2013, it was the 0–3 Steelers versus the 0–3 Vikings at Wembley Stadium in London during the 2013–2014 season. I'm sure the NFL brass were a little bummed that this game meant to further showcase the sport pitted two winless teams playing to salvage a season. Either way, they do seem to be making inroads in England now although the NFL Europe league folded in 2007 after over a decade of play.

American football is tough, seemingly more and more hard hitting, and produces great, tragic, and compelling storylines from Tim Tebow and Ray Lewis to Richard Sherman and Peyton Manning. Sherman's passionate antics made him a household name and sought-after talk show guest in the two weeks between the conference championships and the 2014 Super Bowl. Sherman has passion for the game. I respect that, and I don't really have an issue with him. I just don't care for the way he handled himself after the NFC Championship game. Yes, get pumped up and get excited, but also show that you can control your emotions without putting down everyone else. If you are really that good, why do you need to talk down about everyone else? Leave it on the field. The NFL is trying to promote this culture and brand, and it isn't for me. Why is this important? Ask yourself if that is the type of role model you'd like your children to aspire to. Throwing choking signs at the opposition and screaming into the camera?

And I get it. He may be trying to create Brand Sherman, make the media rounds, get promoted on YouTube, and have every media outlet clamoring for him. After all, NFL careers aren't always long and predictable.

Just ask Tim Tebow. Tim had a remarkable collegiate career, winning two national championships and the Heisman Trophy. His faith-based football at the professional level was inspiring but short-lived.

The NFL on TV: Decline of an Empire?

Not that American football or baseball will need to fall off a bit to make room for soccer, but when I watch parts of NFL games on TV, I realized the NFL is slowly becoming overproduced, corporate, and glossy and feels a little top-heavy. Something about it doesn't feel right. Yet the pace of American football makes the game ideal for broadcasting. The game does have natural stops and starts. And that's not necessarily a bad thing. The commercials during NFL games make it all worthwhile: erectile dysfunction pills; safe, roomy sedans; and pickup trucks that have enough cup holders for the offensive line. Fast-food companies are making containers of food to fit into the cup holders—cups of fried chicken, chicken wings, or chicken fries. What? Yes, chicken fries with a Diet Coke. Various forms of fried chicken aside, nothing says America like a good old-fashioned pickup truck commercial.

"A man."

"A man and his truck."

"A man and his truck mending a fence."

"A man and his truck mending a fence and a runaway calf."

"A man and his truck mending a fence with a heart big enough to search for the calf."

With pouring rain and a tree fallen across the road, a man drives his truck around or over the tree, finds the calf, and tips his cowboy hat to the world. Like a rock, baby. Cue the *Star-Spangled Banner*. I am not making this up.

Soccer is played for forty-five minutes plus stoppage time with no commercial interruptions. So there is no time to get another beer or take a bathroom break. If you step away, you might miss a goal that could decide the game.

Without passionate fans, none of the sponsors would pay top dollar for the commercial spots, so something is clearly working for the NFL. It makes me wonder, though, about the product the networks are trying to enhance with jogging animated robots in full football pads that jump up and down. Helmets slamming into one another and then blowing up? Do these touches enhance the viewing pleasure of an American football game?

I have to apologize to American football. I'm sorry for piling on. Years of frustration from watching just poured out. I honestly haven't watched a complete football game in five years, and I'm okay with it. I don't play fantasy (American) football.

The game is still king in America, and I do enjoy it from time to time. The players who play the game right make it all worthwhile with no showboating and businesslike attitude. Celebrate when you win, not when you get a first down in the second quarter when you are down by seventeen. Do your job, and do it well. Keep calm, cool, and collected. This Bud's for you.

As for the corporate feel? It's fair to say I've been a little harsh. "And that's the half. Stay tuned for the Visa Halftime Show from the KFC Studios live from Disney World with your host Chris Berman brought to you by Cialas and Hair Club for Men."

Disclaimer on this section: I'm not writing this book to beat up on other sports. But the NFL should be concerned that playoff games in 2014 are having a hard time selling out. Would people rather stay home, watch the game on HD, and munch on Tostitos from a bag that didn't cost $10.50?

Holding Interest: Side Games

Both football and American football keep up interest by people playing fantasy football. The NFL, MLB, NBA, FIFA, and Barclays Premier League owe a debt to the creators of fantasy sports. Shows on YouTube and TV are dedicated to picking the best fantasy players and teams. It connects fans to the game in new ways, as they learn about and cheer for players they wouldn't otherwise notice.

My youngest will spend hours researching players, who is trending, who is playing a match against a weak team, and so forth. For the 2013-2014 Barclay's Premier League Season, being a Liverpool fan made picking his fantasy team fun and easy.

"Should I make Luis Suarez or Daniel Sturridge my captain this week?"

But it isn't just him, and it isn't only football.

"I need Manning to toss three TDs today."

"My defense sucks. Why didn't I pick up Baltimore's D? Idiot!"

"RVP! RVP! RVP! I need a hat trick, baby!"

Top fantasy league members meet in Las Vegas to draft players and, of course, party. There is even a National Fantasy Football

Championship. It is a big-time endeavor for those so inclined to go chest deep in that kind of thing.

"El Classico" vs. The Super Bowl

I watched part of Super Bowl XLVIII. When the TV was switched on in my household, the score was already 29–0 in favor of Seattle. It wasn't much of a game. An estimated 110 million people around the world watched the game, which has drawn over 100 million viewers each year since 2010.

But a match that takes place in Spain draws even more viewers. A recent edition in March 2014 drew over 400 million viewers around the world. Real Madrid FC and Barcelona FC were both in contention to win the Spanish League, and this game took on extra meaning. Sometimes, if one team is running away with the league, it has less significance. But when the teams are tied or close on points, late in the season, "El Classico" transcends geography sometimes drawing two to three times a global Super Bowl audience. Barcelona and Real Madrid can also face each other in a variety of other competitions. Less often, but still significant, they can meet in the Copa Del Rey or even Champions League. Now El Classico is being pushed to new heights as it features the two best players of a generation battling on the pitch: Cristiano Ronaldo and Lionel Messi.[19]

---

[19] http://edition.cnn.com/2014/03/23/sport/football/real-madrid-barcelona-clasico/

CHAPTER FOURTEEN

Football: Getting into the Global Game

REAL FOOT + BALL equals soccer, futbol, il calico, and so forth. If you say "soccer" in England, they know what you mean. They may also act slightly offended, wrinkle their nose, and remind you of the proper term, even if the word "soccer" has British Isle roots and some of the commonwealth countries use the term. The game played at levels under the age of eleven is called mini soccer in England, so the term is used, even if it is to describe a junior level of the game. Heck, Australia's national team is called the Socceroos. They cutely combined two words to form an unmistakable marsupial brand. But that is the point. There is the sense that "we invented the game, so call it football. If you don't, you are playing an inferior version of the game."

Alas, my children are huge football fans. They can talk shop with the best of them, especially my older son.

"Good heavens," my wife says, "please talk about something else."

The kids can relate any conversation back to football: tennis, the color pink, Iraq, or anything. One is a Portland Timbers fan, and the other supports Seattle Sounders. Timbers Joey revs up a chainsaw and cuts a slab off a tree when the Timbers score. Paul Bunyan, eat your heart out! And the Sounders Army seemingly grows every game. Seattle draws over forty thousand to each home match.

When we moved to England in 2011, we didn't support any particular English Premier League team. Now, after similar cultural experiences, one of my kids cheers for Tottenham Hotspurs and the other pulls for Liverpool. Tottenham are perennial underdogs with respect to the big English clubs and came tantalizingly close to the final coveted Champions League spot the last two seasons, finishing one point behind Arsenal in the standings this year after getting bumped by Chelsea who won Champions League in 2012 and automatically qualified for the next season.

Clint Dempsey's transfer from Fulham to Tottenham in 2012 solidified my older son's support for the Spurs (along with pressure from certain family members). But the Spurs best player in the 2012–2013 season wasn't American, English, Spanish, or Brazilian. Gareth Frank Bale is a super-fast Welshman who is on the verge of becoming a global superstar. He was a bolt of lightning down the stretch for the Spurs last season, smashing and chipping balls into the back of the net on a weekly basis, keeping Spurs right on the heels of Chelsea in the EPL table. Bale has power and speed, and his game reminds me of LeBron James. He is that good and has sky-high potential.

In the summer of 2013, he became the most expensive footballer ever as Real Madrid agreed to a $120–130 million transfer fee. The Spanish and English press reported different amounts for the "undisclosed price," hence the spread. Rumors suggest it was undisclosed so as not to upstage Real Madrid teammate Chirstiano Ronaldo.

I really don't know why my younger son cheers for Liverpool, but if pressed, I would say that he rebelled against his classmates. After Chelsea won the 2012 Champions League final, every kid in his second-grade class, save one, was wearing Chelsea Blue. My kids' allegiances might also be tied to a fateful day in February 2012. On February 26, we ventured to my aunt and uncle's pub near Wembley Stadium to watch a Premier League match between Spurs and Arsenal. Most of my wife's family is Arsenal supporters. The youngest daughter of the pub owner was engaged to a Spurs fans, and we were invited to come watch the family fireworks that happen during this North London derby. This was one of those matches that invoked plenty of fireworks inside the pub. Spurs scored twice early, only to have Arsenal steamroll them with four straight goals. Mark, the poor Spurs fan, went quickly from quiet jubilation to quiet solitude.

The 2012 Football League Cup Final between Cardiff City and Liverpool was a pivotal moment as well. It was really happenstance that we watched that match as it started shortly after the Arsenal-Tottenham game finished so we stayed in the pub and watched Liverpool win the trophy. It was an exciting match as well with the score tied 1–1. They went into extra time. Liverpool scored in the second half of extra time and tried to hang on, but with three minutes to go, Cardiff found the equalizer setting up penalty drama. Despite the loss, Cardiff was proud to be on the same ground as Liverpool. This is the beauty of the various types of competitions. Cardiff was playing in England's second league at the time, but it had progressed all the way to the final.

Liverpool has Uruguayan international star Luis Suarez. Suarez plays with passion. He plays with abandon, but he also bites players. He and Liverpool captain (and England captain) Steven Gerrard have Liverpool poised to win their first league title in twenty-four years. Neither is bad at taking free kicks either. But Luis Suarez does have a few quirks in his personality and style of play. He defends his goal with his hands. Sometimes, he scores goals with his hands.

After scoring the winning match with an unintentional handball in a league match, he ran over to the crowd and kissed his hand. His intentional handball in the 2010 World Cup to deny Ghana a goal was respectable. Most players would have done the same thing. In fact, his goal line mate on that play also had his arms up. The ball just happened to hit Suarez. It was the World Cup knockout round. If you lose, you go home. Then when Suarez's strange demeanor saw him bite a Chelsea player on the arm, that raised his intrigue even higher. Sadly, not the first time, he was accused of biting a player.

Yet here was a player for the team my son cheered biting a player for the team he loathed. It was a silly act, but the suspension was worse than some nasty, injury-seeking tackles and worse than some players making racist comments. Oh, that's right. Suarez has also been accused of making racist comments. Okay, he's not the best role model, so it's time to move on.

We all support Fulham. They are a short ten-minute train ride to Putney in London from our house, followed by a beautiful walk along the Thames to Craven Cottage. Instead of tailgating in a parking lot, a pregame soccer tradition is the walk to the match. A stroll to a Fulham match is along the River Thames. Fulham play in an old, grand stadium that provides an intimate experience. From Fulham's website, "Resting on the banks of the Thames, Craven Cottage, the oldest football stadium in London, is a must see for any visitor or football fan traveling through London."[20]

Fulham has been a solid mid-table team and has been for quite a few years. (However, they aren't looking really good in 2014, as they are currently at the bottom of the Premier League.) People comment they are a family-friendly venue where home and away supporters can watch the match in harmony. We've seen them play

---

[20] http://www.fulhamfc.com/visit

Chelsea and Everton as well as Stoke, Wolves (sorry about another relegation, Wolves fans), Sunderland, and others at the "Cottage." And yes, we got to see Clint Dempsey play for them before he left for Spurs and then the Sounders.

But most of all, we cheer for the United States. We cheer for the men, women, and U teams. We cheer for American players playing soccer overseas. We cheer for MLS teams to win the CONCACAF Champions League. We cheer for the women to win the Algarve Cup. (This is a tournament that is on my soccer bucket list and should be on yours as well!) I am proud to wear my Stars and Stripes jersey my boys gave me. (And I still think it is the best-looking damn jersey around.) Anytime we see an American playing soccer, we cheer him or her on.

It is not a prerequisite that you need to pick a European football club and follow it, but it does help. It helps when you run into Europeans, Mexicans, and folks from all over the world. You can engage and connect with them, even if you pick one of the heavyweights like Barcelona, Real Madrid, Manchester United, or Bayern Munich.

CHAPTER FIFTEEN

Paying Homage to Messi

I WAS NEVER a Chicago Bulls, nor a particularly big basketball fan, but I did have a Michael Jordan poster in my room that I retrieved from a cereal box promotion. There was something real about fetching the scissors and cutting the box tops, repeating this over the course of a few weeks or months to satisfy the demands of the promotion. It may have made me eat more Cheerios, Special K, or Wheaties, I don't really remember, but it certainly wasn't a sugary cereal mess. One wouldn't mistake this cereal for cookies. It was also a good after-school snack. The end product was five or six pieces of cardboard tops (proof of purchase) stuffed into an envelope with a handwritten address destined for Iowa with hope and a check for $1.95. It was so much more work than downloading an app or screen saver and so much more rewarding. Jordan could fly, and this poster was tangible evidence.

When Michael Jordan was playing in the conference or NBA finals, I paid attention. I remember one particular season working at a greenhouse among acres of color. My radio Walkman broadcasted more color into my ear while tending the greenery and sweeping the floors. Silky smooth Clyde "the Glide" Drexler and the Portland Trail Blazers put up a mighty battle, but Jordan and the Bulls began their reign that year, winning the championship in six games. If a team put together a threatening stretch of play, Michael Jordan always had an answer. When I wasn't working, I would watch him play on TV, stunned at the drive, determination, and general love of the game. He was a special player who captivated all people, not just Bulls fans and not just basketball fans. He was clutch, and he was a champion. I was sad and intrigued when he retired from basketball the first time as he wanted to pursue his first sports love, baseball.

We watched his minor league career with the White Sox farm team, but the magic he showed on the court didn't carry over to the baseball diamond. He is human after all. It didn't matter much in the grand scheme of things. He left baseball after the 1994 season, going back to the Bulls, and won three more championships just like that. Then he really did retire after a brief spell at the Washington Wizards. Michael Jordan transcended the game of basketball and became a global icon.

It is the same with football and Lionel Messi. We've seen many highlights of Messi cutting up Spanish league teams, defeating European powers, and taking it to Brazil's national team. We've watched goals that make you cover your mouth and feel for the defender.

On the rare occasion Barca is losing a league match, Messi digs down, calm resolve comes over his face, and he turns slightly to his teammates with a pass-me-the-ball look. This look also casts a spell on opposition. They expect Messi to deliver. The game slows down for him, and the ball soon goes up the back of the net and then again. Just as a shrug of the shoulder, Messi wins the game, and the broad characteristic Messi smile comes out. You can see the joy of a kid in that smile. The spell is broken, and the defenders wake up, wondering, "What just happened?"

Even when the game is played at normal speeds, the ball is tethered to his foot, and if you give him an inch of space, he will accelerate around you or pop past you and blast a left-footed shot into the corner of the net. How can someone of his stature hammer the ball with such velocity? How can someone be that smart, quick, agile, skilled, and determined? He has the same qualities as MJ. I never saw MJ or Wayne Gretzky play in person. Alaska was a long way from the Lower Forty-Eight for a teenager with no money. I don't regret it, but I also wasn't going to waste the chance to see Messi play.

Barcelona is a short plane ride from London, and we managed to get tickets to a Barcelona-Celtic Champion's League group game in October 2012. I took my kids with me and flew to Barcelona from London with many well-lubricated Celtic fans. Many of the Celtic fans were just happy to be playing Champions League football and were predicting a 4–1 or 5–1 score line. We walked to the Nou Camp, watched, and mingled with the crowds around one of the most famous football grounds in the world. The stadium is the largest in Europe with room for almost a hundred thousand. It is a shrine and futbol temple taken together. Kids the world over know of and dream of playing for Barca someday.

It is also a place where political statements are made. Americans don't always realize that, to many around the world, the football team is also a cultural and political rallying point. The Catalan flag flies freely in Barcelona, and for the 2013–2014 season, Barca's third kit is basically the Catalan flag. "*Mes que un club* (More than a club)."

The streets were lined with fans waiting for the Barcelona players' bus to arrive at the stadium. We were soaking in the atmosphere outside and beaming as we walked in and found our seats. The stadium is massive. What an incredible and intimidating place to play as an away team. As a spectator, you could feel the weight of it all: the history, the desire of millions of kids to play here, the brand of a dominating, silky smooth style of play called tikka takka, and the superstars past and present.

Celtic fought above their weight, as they had all season in the Champions League and even exposed Barcelona a few times. Shockingly, Celtic actually beat Barcelona in Glasgow on the return leg. But this night belonged to Barca. The away crowd would count the number of consecutive passes that Celtic made and started to get excited when they reached eight or nine. Celtic defended well and even scored first. Georgios Samaras headed home a goal off a free kick that meekly bounced in, igniting a near riot from the away fans. We glanced up at the away section, and it looked like pandemonium. Celtic withstood prolonged Barcelona possessions and attacks for long stretches, as Barca just passed the ball around the box without much success. But the final was 2–1 with Barcelona scoring the winner at ninety plus four. It was total domination except for goals. Barcelona won more corners, 15–1, and had more shots on goal, 13–2. It was a decent game, not the greatest, and Messi played well but not spectacularly. Then he didn't need to be spectacular in this game. They knew they would make it out of their group and needed to balance this game against the upcoming league match. None of that mattered. We were paying homage to the greatest soccer player in a generation and maybe of all time.

CHAPTER SIXTEEN

Nightmares and Dreams

MONSTERS SLEEPING UNDER the bed or running out of ice cream, nightmares used to be so innocent. I have terrifying nightmares as an adult. Sometimes I'm naked on stage, or I fell through the rotten floor of an old, creaky Alaskan outhouse. But I have one that takes the cake, and it has nothing to do with ice cream, outhouses, paranormal stuff, alien abduction, or zombies. It's a recurring nightmare in which the Stars and Stripes players hang their heads in seated, sweaty, defeated positions on some hot, humid pitch in Central America, having conceded a late goal to a scrappy opponent that knock us out of WCQ. It almost happened to the Mexican National team.

That's the end. All is lost. The fellowship is over. The dwarves, humans, and elves failed me, and the black knight riding around on some dragon monster just ended it. It doesn't matter if it's in group stages or the final Hexagonal WCQ from our region. We should… no, check that… we have no reason not to qualify. The only other powerhouse (if we can be considered a football powerhouse) in our region is Mexico. As I look up at the scoreboard, it says, "Full Time: Middle America 1–0 USA."

As an American living in England, I will now have to endure the wrath of my friends and family for this painful exit. The wrath will be well deserved. If there were a World Cup for smack talking,

America would be Brazil and Italy combined. The call up to the national smack talking team never came, but my game was solid:

"We finished top of the group ahead of England in South Africa 2010. And we advanced from our Group of Death in Brazil. Get me another pint mate!

"We beat Italy in Italy in 2012. We beat Mexico at Azteca while they were on a victory tour weeks after they took home Olympic gold from London where they beat Brazil in the final. America is for real. I'm not sure why more Americans aren't playing for Champions League teams."

"Do I need to remind you of England's record against the USA in World Cup games?"

(For the home gamers, England has no wins, one tie, and one loss against the States!)

"Seventeen goals for Dempsey in Premier League games, and none of them were gimmie penalties. The only Englishman with more goals was Rooney. Deuce is a beast"

"Did you read the book *Why England Lose*? In England, it's called *Soccernomics*."

"Robert Green is an American hero."

"A 2–2 draw in Russia late in 2012. The same Russian team that had allowed one goal in 2014 WCQ until then. Not bad…"

And they get sharper as the pints go down. And really, smack talking isn't a sport in England as it is in the States, so it's pretty mild. Making fun of Kirby Puckett in the Twin Cities or John Elway anywhere near the Rocky Mountains is a different story. And don't get me started on the Yankees. (Even Jeter is fair game.)

"Shannon?" I try to get a response from my wife to make sure it wasn't real.

"Wha?" she replies.

"I just needed some water." I lied, wiping the sweat from my forehead. It was just a dream. In 2013, we finished at the top of the Hex.

Robert Green

Playing goalkeeper can be thankless. Save after save, brave jumps, and punches yet, you can still end up the goat. I include this little section about Robert Green under the nightmare category. His gift allowed Clint Dempsey and the United States to draw England 1–1 in the opening group game for each country in the 2010 World Cup, but it is still a nightmare, a "howler" as they are called. I'm a fan of the game and don't like to see players make horrific blunders. His error will forever be remembered. England finished second in the group and still made it to the knockout round, but Robert Green didn't play again in the 2010 World Cup.

Late into the game, he did make a tremendous save on a streaking Jozy Altidore as he punched the ball onto the post, preserving the draw. Thankfully, he has been called up since then and even kept a clean sheet for England. He now plays for Queen's Park Rangers in England's second league after they were relegated from the Premier League in the 2012–2013 season, but I doubt he'll be on the plane to Brazil.

Croatia and Prague

In 2012, we found ourselves in Prague for a couple days on our way to a wonderful holiday in Croatia. Euro 2012 was in full swing, and we got to witness the passion firsthand. In Prague, squares were decked out with big screens so the masses could watch, drink, and revel together. The Czech Republic received an opening game beating by the Russians and then regrouped to beat Greece and Poland, finishing top of the group on six points, albeit with a negative goal differential. Their success was short-lived as they fell victim to Ronaldo and Portugal in the next round.

When we arrived in Croatia, the Croatian team was alive in Group C, a Group of Death that included defending World Cup and European Cup Champions Spain and perennial powerhouse Italy, along with the Republic of Ireland. Croatia dismissed Ireland 3–1 and then drew Italy 1–1, setting up a showdown with Spain. A 1–1 draw with Spain would see them through to the next round.

While eating at a pizza place in Brac, we watched Croatia valiantly go down to a mighty European power. The server, bartender, cook, and so forth slowed the service whenever Croatia was on the attack. It's part of the culture, and we were on vacation. We had favorite tonic in hand, and our skin was expelling that day's soaked sun rays back into the beautiful Croatian night. The small cafés around the Sutivan waterfront and open plazas had put TVs outside so no diners or passersby would miss the action of Euro 2012. Would Spain repeat? It seemed inevitable, and it was of course. But still, the sense was optimistic. (Like a Pirates or Royals fan on Opening Day, only those teams have no chance. And Croatia can at least look at Greece's recent success for hope!)

Croatia was playing well and has a handful of internationals playing at the highest levels around Europe. Along with the above-mentioned optimism, you got the sense that, to the locals, the best was yet to come for Croatia. Maybe not in Euro 2012 or Brazil 2014 but beyond. Perhaps after being admitted to the EU. They can play.

Alas, the next day, fresh from a Croat departure from Euro 2012, I found myself, my wife, and assorted company on a winery tour, learning of the Plavac Mali grape. A former professional footballer and his wife ran her family's generational wine business. That lightheaded feeling that comes with three or four glasses of clean, fresh wine allows fun thoughts to escape into the evening air.

Upon hearing that our hosts were former footballers and WAGs and wanting to converse, my lovely wife asked who our winemakers were cheering for in EuroVisions.

At the time, I had a vague idea of what EuroVisions were. It's some sort of continental *X Factor* competition pitting amateur singers and performers against each other. It was probably as foreign to me as Euro 2012 was to my lovely wife. Assorted company had to remind her gently that Croatia was eliminated the previous night in the Euro 2012 football tournament, not EuroVision. Our hosts took minimal offense and probably chalked it up to a lost-in-translation episode or an excusable American transgression.

My wife understands sports. She is a good athlete herself and has great respect for the New York Yankees, which she inherited from her Italian, New Yorker father. Even though she is not a dyed-in-the-wool sports fan, she will watch the Super Bowl and loves the Olympics. After living with three rabid football fans, she is learning quite a bit and we can now safely call her a football fan.

Dreams

In the spring of 2013, we took our kids to South Africa for holiday with a family friend. We went on safari in Kruger National Park and saw baby leopards, elephants, and all the normal, amazing animals the country has to offer. While at the safari camp, after lunch, my older son and I would play a version of football with the locals and workers. Played during the hottest part of the day, the game involved two teams of ten to twelve on a squared pitch of varying terrain and grass length. There were no goals. It was just a possession game. Switching from holders to defenders all the time was draining. Once your team was back on the ball, you had to go very wide out into space, not toward any goal.

None of these guys had any formal football training. Their skills were developed on the dirt pitches away from the structure of the modern game. That bred a creative and very fast type of football. There weren't any dirty tackles or shoving, just a normal amount of shoulder bumping. Quick turns and one-touch quick release passes dominated the game. I was amazed at how graceful and flowing it was. They have played this type of game together for a long time, and the players knew the types of runs the others were going to make. I won't say that I fit in with the style after four or five days, but I did start to figure out the tempo and how I could fit in. Granted, it required me being fifteen years younger and fifteen pounds lighter to do so and then just on the fringes.

Sometimes, the glare of the midday African sun was too much, and the Alaskan in me would start melting. I took a seat as play continued, watching the faces of the players and the joy the game brought them. The football connected us. It is a wonderful memory.

As I write this following the death of Nelson Mandela, I fully understand the power of sport to change a nation. Rugby and soccer have rightfully been used to heal the damage done by generations of oppression in South Africa. On the ride back to Cape Town from Robben Island, Cape Town Stadium (formerly Green Point Stadium) sits on the eastern end of the city, a palpable modern monument to the power of sport. FIFA did well to give the tournament to this deserving nation.

Azteca 2009

Even a loss can be a memorable moment for fans. One of the contributors to this book, Mike Hood, wrote about his experience in Mexico City at the USA Mexico WCQ in 2009.

The Night Before

We walk through the streets of Mexico City, taking in the sights, scenes, and smells. Downtown Mexico City is a colorful and bustling place. It is easy to forget about the crime you read about back home. We all congregate in a generic sports bar in the Zona Rosa section of the city the night before the big game at Azteca. One by one, the bar fills with Yanks wearing red, white, and blue. The Mexican bartenders stare at us and have puzzled look on their faces.

"Wait? There are Americans who like futbol?"

This is what makes following the USNMT so fun. It feels like the Fourth of July every time we get together. Friends, new and old, come from all corners of America: sharing stories, drinking beer, catching up, waxing nostalgic about past games (Dos a Cero!), and, most importantly, getting fired up for Azteca. USA! USA! USA! Our usual repertoire of greatest hits is pumping. It's like a drunken choir practice. Estados Unidos! Estados Unidos! The more Coronas that go down, the louder the singing gets. At this point in the night, anything but victory seems impossible tomorrow. We are ready to witness history and conquer almighty Azteca together.

The Pregame

It is an abnormal day in Mexico City. The temperature is mild, and some breezes are clearing the air. Air pollution isn't as bad as expected. We meet at the hotel, and our group slowly gathers. The plan is to take the subway to the game. Our parade of red, white, and blue starts its procession through the streets. "USA!" chants slowly commence. Our hangovers make way for the adrenaline. Cars honking, street vendors whistling at us, young kids pointing, and people taking pictures meet us. It's all good-natured fun like the previous night. Our groups pile into multiple subway cars, yelling, "Estados Unidos!" The Mexicans are amused and a bit bewildered.

They have the same annoyed look as the bartenders from the night before.

"How did we get stuck with these gringos?"

We exit the subway and take in the first glimpse of Azteca. It's a striking sight. The stadium is a massive and dramatic structure of concrete that resembles an ancient Mayan temple. Everybody breaks off to go explore the myriad of food vendors and merchandise stands. A few of us hang out next to the fence around the corner from the entrance. I decide to jump up on the wall near the front gate to take a picture of the crowd. For the fortress that Azteca is, the wall surrounding the stadium is shockingly accessible and easy to climb.

I make my way up and stroll around the corner. I am surprised to see thousands of fans. A sea of black hair and green jerseys is waiting for the doors to open. Dressed head to toe in red, white, and blue, my presence ignites a loud reaction from the crowd, and whistles, horns, and screams meet me. The projectiles are launched, and I take a quick picture. As I wave to the crowd, I get a few hundred middle fingers in return. Welcome to Azteca.

The Stadium

The seventy-three hundred feet of altitude becomes noticeable on our long ascent up the ramps to our seats. We huff and puff and finally reach the top of Azteca. Our special visiting fan section resembles a penitentiary and comes complete with a chain-link fence and riot police on both sides. From here, the vantage point of the stadium is sprawling. You feel like you are closer to heaven than the field. If this were acutely a Mayan temple, we would be sitting in the area closest to the gods where the victims are sacrificed. It feels appropriate.

Out of nowhere, the beer vendors show up and deliver large warm cups of *cerveza*. Coincidentally, the trash talk and unfriendly banter between the tiny contingency of Yanks and the growing populations of neighboring Mexicans on the other side of the fence begins. It becomes rather entertaining to both sides as we have time to kill before the kickoff. Our exchange consists of insults in broken English and Spanish. However, you don't really need to know either language to understand what was being said.

It is amazing to watch the stadium grow and the noise build while we sit for a couple hours. Azteca slowly takes on a life of its own. Once the teams enter the field, the atmosphere reaches a fever pitch, and the place is literally buzzing. It sounds like a massive beehive.

We sing our national anthem first, and the surrounding fans whistling and jeering us instantly drowned us out. The only time you will hear the cheap Mexican horns stop and all of the commotion halt is during the Mexican national anthem. The magnitude of the Mexican national anthem is astounding as their pride resonates throughout Azteca.

The Food

The many food vendors start to visit us. The Azteca food and beverage selection consists of all the usual stadium staples that we see at home, but there are also bizarre offerings like hot cup o'noodles. If I were a young enterprising food vendor at Azteca, I would give all the Americans the following advice, "Whatever you don't buy from me will get thrown at you by the guys on the other side of the fence in the next ninety minutes, so stock up, amigo."

The Game

The kickoff ensues, and there is a big roar from the crowd. There is nervous energy amongst the American supporters. The focus on both sides of the fence finally turns to the game. In the eighteenth minute, Charlie Davies scores a sublime goal off a beautiful pass from Landon Donovan. It is pure pandemonium in our section. All you can hear in the stadium is our celebration. Jubilation. Hugging. Jumping. Screaming. This is what we made the journey for. For many, the celebration is cut short. The seventy-three hundred feet kicks in, and we are sucking oxygen. My head hurts, I lose my breath, and I feel as if I am going to pass out. I grip the post in the aisle next to me and take a seat. When I glance around, I see others with the same dazed look.

The game starts again, and the buzz returns to Azteca. With that comes the beginning of the perpetual shower of beers tossed into our section. Israel Castro answers for Mexico in the twentieth minute, and Azteca is rocking. It is now a torrential downpour of beer, food, and filthier flying objects. A guy behind me shrieks and throws his hands in the air. His friends are laughing as he complains that he just got hit in the back with something that feels a lot warmer than beer. As the game goes on, it gets tougher and tougher to stay completely focused on the field. With so many projectiles whizzing by our heads, you have to keep one eye on your surroundings. It feels like an epic food fight and dodgeball game has broken out.

At first, many of the American fans try to ignore what was going on. Many folks reach their limit and fight back. The heated exchange accelerates. Miguel Sabah scores for Mexico in the eighty-second minute, the situation is now out of control. A US fan behind us has a two-inch gash in his face from a large piece of ice that was thrown. We put an incredible amount of faith in the riot police, thinking they will be able to protect us if something worse happens. You can tell by the guard's facial expressions that they are concerned, not just for us but for them, too. Mexican fans are now trying to climb the fence to come into our area. With eight minutes left to play, the head of police starts yelling at everyone to evacuate our section because it is not safe.

The Walk of Shame

The final whistle blows, and I look around to see that police have already evacuated half of our section. We begin our descent down the maze of ramps inside the stadium. Police stop the Mexicans from exiting at every intersection, and they yield to us. Thousands of raucous fans, backed up the ramps as far as the eye can see, meet us. People are leaning over, throwing beer, and trying to spit on us. We have now entered something that closely resembles hell. There is really nothing you can do except walk as quickly as possible.

As we approach the ground level, hundreds of police make a rectangular-shaped human shield for all of the Americans to enter. The Mexican onlookers build around us as the fans are allowed to exit the stadium behind us. The exchange of words between the fans gets worse, and large pieces of broken asphalt are tossed into our section. A few of us decide that is it safer to stand close to the guards as the police start to move us toward the exit.

As the police barricade inches along, an intense argument breaks out between two fans. Out of the corner of my eye, a Mexican throws a punch directed at an American next to me. He misses and hits one of the riot police in the side of the head. Without hesitation, the policeman unleashes his baton and take a swipe at the Mexican fan's face. It is a clean blow to the nose, and blood is everywhere. The Mexican drops to the ground with both hands covering his face. The expressionless policeman keeps moving.

A couple hours after leaving our seats, we finally make it out of the stadium gates. Most of the Mexican crowd has dispersed, but police are still escorting us. Concerned with our safety, they will not let us go to the Azteca subway station. We are wandering through the parking lot aimlessly, and our final destination is still unclear. Eventually, we make it to the corner of the parking lot where more police and a line of large paddy wagons greeted us.

One by one, we all climb aboard. It is questionable whether this bus will be taking us home or to the police station. We finally confirm that they will be taking us to a subway station far away so we do not overlap with the Mexican fans leaving the game. For the first time since we arrived at Azteca, we can finally sit back and relax for a moment. You can hear the disbelief, exhaustion, and amusement in the voices and stories being shared. The bus driver hits the ignition, and the energy in the bus changes. Smiles break out all around. A loud "USA! USA!" chant starts.

We all start banging on the walls and break into, "We're going home in a Mexican paddy wagon! We're going home in a Mexican paddy wagon!"

The buses start making their way through the Azteca gridlock with the help of the police escort. The police on motorcycles and onlookers sitting in their cars are staring at us and shaking their heads. It is a surreal and unforgettable moment. Everybody in the bus is laughing deliriously. A couple of American flags make their way through the bars in the bus window, and they are waving as we exit the Azteca parking lot.

"We are going home in a Mexican paddy wagon!"

CHAPTER SEVENTEEN

Economics and Sport

MONEY, MONEY, MONEY. It can be a plague for sports: out-of-control player salaries, sky-high ticket prices, league bureaucrats trying to figure out schemes to bring about a little parity, and teams on the verge of bankruptcy. As the game becomes more global, the superstars can be marketing dreams, and they can be worth the huge investments to the rich clubs. Clubs can leverage the best, Messi and Ronaldo, to sell jerseys and grow committed fan bases around the world. When you see $100-million transfer fees, carefully calculated marketing plans are certainly in place to sell that player to a very wide audience and recoup some of that cost immediately but also over decades through new generations of loyal and committed fans.

Think about whom you see in the ads for upcoming matches. It's not FC Barcelona versus Real Madrid. It's Messi, Neymar, and FC Barca taking on Ronaldo and Real Madrid. Of if you prefer the EPL, it's RVP, Rooney, and ManU taking on Mesut Ozil and Arsenal. Clubs are paying for more than just the skill on the pitch. They are paying for all the revenue that comes from the skill on the pitch. The game has come a long way from being a political arena, a place to make a statement. It still happens, though.

But a few things do impact what a die-hard free market capitalist might take issue with. If a factory isn't economical anymore, it can be closed, moved, or retooled. The workers of the unions will embrace none of which, but in the end, the bottom line wins out. Not so with sports teams, and certainly even less with FCs in Europe. The first is the culture and community of the sport. The humble owners, the good ones, talk about being only a custodian of the team that are merely hanging on to the reins for a while, ensuring the sustainability of the club for the next generations. The good ones aren't government-made billionaires who want to own a club as a toy, spending money and making snap decisions. But those are few and far between. Sometimes you can catch glimpses of the owners sitting in a box high above the pitch on match day, trying to stay out of the spotlight. They are on another level even than the players.

I'm reminded of a quote from Chris Rock. "Shaquille O'Neal is rich. The guy who pays his salary is wealthy."[21]

To most of us, the players are rich and on another level, and to them, the owners are another few rungs up the ladder. However, in Europe, one cannot simply buy a club and decide to move it or just terminate it and sell off the land assets to a superstore chain without a massive fight from the fans and local councils.

The clubs in England have history, and they are embedded in the local culture more than any sport. I'm not talking about faded pictures of past glory days hanging in the local pubs. I'm talking about groups of true working-class people starting a club many decades ago. The bonds between players and fans were forged in sweat on the pitch, in the pub, and on the job. They worked together and then went to the stadiums together, celebrated, and cried together. The players and fans shared the experience, and the game was certainly approachable. This history is as firm as the ground. You can't move Liverpool FC to another town. You'd have

---

[21] http://peterfaur.com/2014/04/29/the-difference-between-rich-and-wealthy#axzz32DAEwNjd

to move the entire town. Liverpool is Liverpool. It part of the soul of the city.

The clubs are a part of the fabric of the communities, and it is very painful to move elsewhere. It's not impossible because it rarely does happen, and the bitterness lasts for at least a generation. AFC Wimbledon is a notable example of a club that moved, and it involved a commission, ticked off fans, encompassed a threat of bankruptcy, and incurred blood, sweat, and tears.

Another popular idea to raise money for a FC is to sell shares to the public. Manchester United is listed on the New York Stock Exchange. But an absolute last resort, I mean, after bloody boardroom scuffles, is to move a FC to another area, town, city, or region with more profit potential. It happens more frequently in America. Cleveland Browns? Baltimore Ravens? Why are the Los Angeles Lakers called the Lakers? Utah Jazz? Los Angeles Dodgers? And many more. Many teams moved west with the growth of America. We embrace the idea of free market enterprise, and we are more willing than European FCs to move teams.

Obama Is (Not) a Socialist and Taxes!

This certainly isn't a political book, but I do get a kick out of people when they call Obama a socialist. I usually respond by saying that, if you took Obama and put him in Europe, he'd be a moderate, perhaps even conservative. In 2012, France actually elected a socialist president who wants to impose a 75 percent super tax on income over a million euros ($1.3 million).

This brings me to an economic point that has thrown France and its football leagues into a tizzy. You picked up a football book, and you are reading about taxes. How boring, but please hear me out because it is an important point. Monaco is a sovereign state with a really good football team, AS Monaco FC. They play in the top league in France. Their owner, Dmitry Rybolovlev, bought 66 percent of the club in December 2011. After winning promotion back into France's top league, Monaco went on a spending spree to secure top players, including Portuguese international Joao Moutinho and Columbian striker Radamel Falcao.

The issue is that Monaco's players aren't subject to France's income tax laws, thanks to a tax treaty between the two countries. France's governing football authority can't issue court rulings on Monaco, but they have formally asked Monaco FC to move its offices to Paris so they would be subjected to France's, not Monaco's, income tax laws. Monaco declined and filed a suit. Why should Monaco be punished just because of a political decision in Paris? If France doesn't want to honor its treaties, it should change them.

"It is very clear it will be much more expensive if they have to move all their staff, including players, to France. It means they will all have to pay French taxes," says Ms Moyersoen, who is also president of the International Association of Football Lawyers (AIAF).[22]

I know what you are thinking now. An international association of football lawyers? When is their Christmas party, and can I get a ticket?

In January 2014, France and the club reached an agreement. "Out of concern for the equality and balance of the competition, AS Monaco is committed to paying a voluntary, fixed and definitive sum of €50 million to the LFP," the league said in a Friday statement, "and will withdraw their plea to the Council of State."[23]

Voluntary indeed. Definitive for now.

---

[22]   www.bbc.com, August 14, 2013.

[23]   http://www.ligue1.com/ligue1/article/statement-on-monaco-agreement.htm

One Billion Dollars Borrowed

I'm sure we will see the first billion-dollar player in my kids' lifetime. As crazy as it sounds, someone will come along and transform the sport... again. Imagine if Pelé were playing today and he was head and shoulders above everyone else like he was in his heyday. Roman Abromovich would call up Putin and ask for a loan if needed. A billion for Pelé? Sure.

Roman: "Hello, Vlady. How is things? Can I get a loan for one billion?"

Putin: "Sure, Roman. As long as you can give Dimitri a job. I'm thinking president of Chelsea FC. It would only be for a few years, and you'd really be in control."

Simple Math

The rich get richer. The economics of wealth inequality apply to football teams. If teams increase their budgets 15 percent from one year to the next, then the rich will just get richer and spend more. It's simple math. A $200,000 budget becomes $230,000, but a $1.0 million budget becomes $1.15 million. This is true in many aspects of society, not just football teams. A further problem arises when teams seemingly have unlimited budgets. The easiest target is Chelsea.

A Russian who came into his money through questionable tactics owns the Blues, but that isn't under indictment here. In order to examine the economics of the game, we need to understand the unquantifiable. How much is an owner willing to spend to win UEFA Champions League? Surely he won't get a proper return on his investment. It's just jewelry for the owner and ecstasy for the longtime fan. The fan has invested some money but far more emotional capital, and that is the return they are seeking. The fan isn't going to get a financial reward if his or her team wins. He or she is just going to feel joy (unless, of course, he or she makes a wager). People, companies, and football clubs can all go under. For sports clubs, usually you hear about a club struggling to pay its players due to someone borrowing a bunch of money, paying silly salaries, and then wishing and hoping for a promotion or some payout. Who does the cash flow analysis when they take on the loans? Do they consider a scenario that maybe... just maybe... they don't get promoted or the star signing is injured? Or is it all pie in the sky, rainbows, and unicorn dreams? Ticket sales up 15 percent, food and drink sales up 20 percent, and jersey and branded merchandise up 30 percent—let's borrow even more! Then money will be flowing in.

I get it. There could be a little bit of an upward spiral. The club starts winning, and marginal, fair-weather fans come back. Attendance goes up. There's more money, more signings, and potential promotion. And when it happens, the payday could be huge, but this tends to happen far less frequently than people think. When clubs to get into financial trouble, they can approach the lenders and ask for forgiveness and time. In many cases, they give up ownership.

ACKNOWLEDGEMENTS

A huge thank you to my family for providing inspiration and lively football discussions. Special thanks to Tony Finn and Paul Caligiuri for their efforts and contributions. To Kenna Bates and Christopher Constant for the cover art. Mike Hood, Kelly Fricks and Michael Temlett for their stories and belief. I would also like to thank all of the people on trains, in pubs, at matches, on football pitches around Europe, South Africa, Brazil and The United States that helped me realize this book was not only possible, but needed. To my American Outlaw London family for sharing the passion, especially Nathen McVittie, Dylan Glass, Jermaine Martin, Diego Picon, Max Singer and Nate Shoemate. (Shoutout to Brookhattan FC) Lastly, thank you to all the players, parents and coaches that understand and believe in the potential of The Beautiful Game in the United States of America.

THE END-GAME

Here we are, a collection of immigrants from around the world, yet we have shunned the sport we were meant to play. My ancestry is Belgian, Russian, and Slovak. My wife is Irish-Italian. America is equipped to support soccer at the national level, and it will be revealed over the next few decades. We shouldn't think of it as "not our sport" just because it took a backseat to other sports for a bit. Nor do we need to be cappuccino drinkers in high fashion to embrace it. The game is American. Perhaps it won't be until Americans ask for time off from work to watch World Cup matches, as they do in Germany, but it will come.

We don't need to embrace the invented domestic games anymore as a form of rebellion. Heck, America has advanced globalization more than any other country and should be prepared to realize the cultural impacts brought home.

And buried deep down in the psyche of the American sports fan is the feeling that we could be great at soccer. We can and are competing with the best national teams, but the American fan, still skeptical and suspicious, isn't ready to commit yet.

America has shown that it has passion for the sport. Two important examples are the New York Cosmos and the 1994 World Cup hosted by the United States. The average attendance for the

World Cup was almost seventy thousand per match, long before the MLS was on solid footing demonstrating.

With some of the new MLS teams, people have a chance to be a part of the history and to help grow the sport. It is why David Beckham brought his game to America and why he is staying on to help bring a team to Miami. Becks says, "I want to create a team that is personal to me. I know this city is ready for soccer, football, and this is going to be successful... I want to make it my own team."[24] That is the appeal. Becks knows that soccer is here to stay. He's experienced it as a player and now hopes to be successful as an investor.

We like seeing the medal count at the Olympics, and we love the underdog story. And we certainly love cheering for Team USA. When Landon Donovan scored that goal, it was crucial, and it showed that America was not only watching but also waking up to the beautiful game.

If you are feeling called into action, you can:

- bring your Don't Tread on Me flag to a match;
- get a scarf;
- sing, chant, bang the drums, and cheer;
- join a local team and play;
- get your kids playing; or
- get involved in a local club team at any level.

---

[24] www.cnn.com, February 5, 2014.

ADDITIONAL READING

Bondy, Filip. *Chasing the Game: America and the Quest for the World Cup*, Da Capo Press, Cambridge, MA 2010

Burns, Jimmy. *La Roja: How Soccer Conquered Spain and How Spanish Soccer Conquered the World*, Nation Books, New York, 2012

Conn, David. *The Beautiful Game: Searching for the Soul of Football*, Yellow Jersey Press, London, 2005

Hornby, Nick. *Fever Pitch*, Gollancz Press, London, 1992

Kuper, Simon, and Stefan Szymanski. *Why England Lose: And Other Curious Football Phenomena Explained* (*Soccernomics* in America), Harper Collins, London, 2010

Wilson, Jonathan. *Inverting the Pyramid: The History of Football Tactics*. Orion, London 2009

Made in the USA
San Bernardino, CA
18 November 2014